Revelation 3:20 & 21

20 Behold (Here I am) I stand at the door and knock. If anyone hears my voice and opens the door, I will come in and eat with that person and they with me. 21 To the one who is victorious, I will give the right to sit with me on my throne, just as I was victorious and sat down with my Father on His throne.

There Is A Doorway...

Rick L. Johnson

ISBN 978-1-68517-532-0 (paperback)
ISBN 979-8-88685-874-7 (hardcover)
ISBN 978-1-68517-533-7 (digital)

Copyright © 2022 by Rick L. Johnson

All rights reserved. No part of this publication may be reproduced, distributed, or transmitted in any form or by any means, including photocopying, recording, or other electronic or mechanical methods without the prior written permission of the publisher. For permission requests, solicit the publisher via the address below.

Christian Faith Publishing
832 Park Avenue
Meadville, PA 16335
www.christianfaithpublishing.com

Printed in the United States of America

Table of Contents

Preface v
Opening vii
Chapter One—Foundational Information and Author's
    Experiences 1
Chapter Two—Milk and Honey First 30
Chapter Three—The Good Shepherd 63
Chapter Four—We Are Saved by Grace through Faith 89
Chapter Five—The Doorway 159

Preface

This book is a letter to all my brothers and sisters in Christ Jesus, both current and potential! God is love. This effort was driven out of the zeal received from revelations of God from His living word to us. A lifelong journey of discovery of oneself and the quest of finding God. I have carried an interest to write a book of significance since I was eighteen. This has evolved through four or five idea changes over the many years into this worthiest of efforts. Different versions through different periods or stages have honed my target down to the one we now have here. Worth noting is the evolution of the subject matter and its phases and tailoring over the many years. To realize and fulfill my long-sought-after goal. This book had several previous beginnings, all of which were a preparation or prestaging for the actual intended book. Here listed are the conceived titles of the stories or works that I had entertained in my earlier attempts. They chronicle and reveal a contributing insight.

1. At eighteen years old, "The Apocalyptic Warrior"
2. At approximately twenty-eight to thirty years of age, "Rich Man, Poor Man"
3. At approximately forty-five to forty-six years old, "You Are Only Going Where You Are Headed"
4. At approximately fifty to fifty-one years old, "A Small Slice of American Pie"
5. At fifty-two to fifty-six years old, "The Sage Welder"
6. At approximately fifty-eight to sixty years old, "There Is A Doorway"

I had hoped that in whatever effort that I undertook, it would express my knowledge and appreciation of God, which has grown exponentially over time, along with my study of His word and consequently my Faith, specifically to spotlight, glorify, and extoll God's being, Word, and love for us. This is a book not like many others, being simply about my hobbies or sidebar interests. It is consequential. It is about life, reality, love, and our existence—the causation and purpose. Jesus Christ is God, God the Father, God the Son, and God the Holy Spirit—one being, three similitudes. He is literally the very *Grace* of God personified. He laid down His divinity during His earthly walk to pick it back up after His resurrection. This book is the evidence of that and the power contained therein and is what I have been invited to receive and how I have tapped into and am now sustained by. Amen.

I, Rick L. Johnson, have penned this book to disclose valuable knowledge and revelation received from God's Word, the Holy Bible. This work is purposed to coincide with and to be the official launch of the Ricardo Da Vinci Ministries—a ministry founded on and teaching the *Love, Grace,* and *Peace* of Jesus Christ, as I have been called to share. I am a sexagenarian from Delawarean whose desire to glorify God, was born after the truth of Jesus Christ had been more fully revealed to me.

Opening

The biblical information and knowledge of God in this book is the evolving result of a fifty-year journey of discovery in my life and of the Bible. There will be information about (the author) me, where it is relevant. The emphasis of this journey is not to be centered on me rather on the revelations of a life's search for enlightenment and the path of discovery in this quest. Yes, to even know the "unknowable" God. Indeed, it is quite a lofty reach. It truly has been less of a search and more of a leading. I would like to describe it primarily as following a crumb trail.

By God's Grace, I have been blessed with an intellectual curiosity to not be afraid to ask and seek answers to the big questions that are to be discovered through God's Word. Along with, thankfully, being blessed with the resilience to not rule out God or to give up on understanding our existence and creator. I feel there has been an element of Him leading or seeking me out that has enhanced my search along the way. Now my personal story is not that unique, not even exceptional, and is not the focus of this composition on God. But that my blessings from God have been for certain above average. The glass is way over half full. For *little* becomes much when God is in it. This I know, and it is rather the fact that my personal story is average, concerning my background, my formative years, and my surroundings, that the weight, value, and the merit of this knowledge of God and enlightenment gain traction, once revealed to me by the Holy Spirit through the Bible.

After many years of going to church and of Bible reading and studying, although I was compiling knowledge, wisdom, and historical information, there was a major disconnect or lack of continuity. As if there were a veil over my understanding, a blocking of clarity of the Holy Scriptures; even with constant and persistent study, true revelation had eluded me.

One of the most astounding aspects of all this is that after years of wrong teachings, which led to some wrong or inaccurate understanding and resulted in wrong thinking, I was still able to lay a foundation, gain knowledge, and compile godly wisdom to a point that the Holy Spirit determined that I was ripe for the revealing of the mysteries of, the reason for, and the cause of this existence and our reality. This all-illuminating revelation has been electrified by the teachings of Peter and primarily Paul and the apostle John and the Acts written by Luke in the New Testament of the Holy Scriptures, where the new and more complete understanding has been revealed that it is a continuation and ultimate fulfillment of the Old Testament and there was no actual disconnect, as is historically and traditionally implied. Rather, it is a continuation and establishment of His *Law* of the *Grace* (and *Peace*) and the *Truth* of Jesus Christ and Him crucified, a continuity that many miss and perceive wrongly that one is irrelevant of the other and that, at that time, the Mosaic Law was fulfilled and replaced by Jesus Christ and His finished work at the cross, where the Law of His Grace and Peace, the true gospel, were permanently established—thus, nailing it, "the Law" (the Ten Commandments) and all our condemnation from that dispensation to the cross, removing it (our condemnation, any need for penance, and all enmity from God) with Jesus Christ having paid the price for our redemption, as it was designed and intended by God to do, reconciling us back to the Father, and as it says in Colossians 2:13–15, which states:

> When you were dead in your sins and in the uncircumcision of your flesh, God made you alive with Christ. He forgave us all our sins, Having canceled the charge of our legal indebtedness, which stood against us and condemned us; He has taken it away, nailing it to the Cross.

THERE IS A DOORWAY...

> And having disarmed the powers and authorities,
> He made a public spectacle of them, triumphing
> over them by the Cross.

After many years of meditating on the how and the why, my seeking God, and my searching for the knowledge of Him in His word are what I believe the Holy Spirit responded to, coupled with my new reinvigorated search and zeal to know the complete truth and get closer to God. For the more I read, heard, and studied, the more my Faith in God was built up, delivering me to the point where He allowed me to see it, the *big picture*.

It was through this revelation of God's amazing Grace, His mercy, His undeserved kindness, His favor, and His eternal love, even His radical love for us, me, that the missing pieces to the greatest mysteries of our reality were delivered to me, supplying me with His *Word* to piece together and understand the true gospel of God and Jesus Christ, delivering spiritual answers, and unlocking the mysteries and ultimate purpose of our existence, reality, and universe. In this book, I will seek zealously to deliver and expound on these lofty proclamations using the word of God in scripture. That this undertaking might possibly glorify God and get possibly even if only one person to read their Bible and to seek and possibly receive all or any of this most profound knowledge of God and His wisdom; then, I will be able to say that my effort toward this goal will have been worthwhile. Father God, I pray in Jesus's name, amen.

There Is A Doorway…

Chapter 1

The Beginning

Foundational and Historical Information and the Author's Background, Insights, and Experiences

In John 1:1–14, it states:

> In the beginning was the Word, and the Word was with God, and the Word was God. He was with God in the beginning. Through him all things were made; without Him nothing was made that has been made. In him was life, and that life was the light of all mankind. The light shines in the darkness, and the darkness has not overcome it. There was a man sent from God, whose name was John. He came as a witness to testify concerning that light, so that through him all might believe. He himself was not the light; He came only as a witness to that light. The true light that gives light to everyone was coming into the world. He was in the world and though the world was made through him, the world did not recognize him. He came to that which was his own, but his own did not receive him. Yet to all who did receive him, to those who believed in

his name, he gave the right to become children of God-Children born not of natural descent, nor of a human decision, or a husband's will, but born of God. The Word became flesh and made his dwelling among us. We have seen his glory, the glory of the one and only Son, who came from the Father, full of Grace and Truth.

There is a lot of information that I am going to unload in this chapter. For this is knowledge and information that I am recalling from a lifetime of study into the Word of God—that is, His Holy Bible along with my developmental experiences. Being raised Methodist, I was learning about God and His word, the Bible, since I was a youngster of about four or five years old. I can remember the foundational teachings from just a little guy. I was singing the songs in church ("Jesus Loves Me") about Jesus and God and growing in the knowledge of His word up through church and reading on up through to just before my early teenage years. After years of Sunday school and being taught in church, through the little coloring pictures and some of the stories that were taught in the Sunday school classes, a foundation was beginning to be laid.

We moved to another part of town. In the area that we lived in, there was a Baptist church just about 150 yards from my father's property. Initially, we continued to go to our original Methodist Church close to the house where we lived previously. Unfortunately, over the next few years, divorce would overtake our family. Tough times for sure, but with this, like most things, I never decided to throw a pity party for myself or my situation or to believe that I was the "lone ranger" and the only one suffering such difficulties. I believe this is a result of the concept that I mentioned in my introduction about my perception of the glass always being more than half full. I would like to suggest, and soundly so, that this is a direct result of my awareness of God's favor on my life, whether I understood it or not, from a very early age.

Prior to my parents' difficult split, there was an out-of-the-ordinary situation where my dad received all six of us kids into his custody, a gargantuan task for anyone given the same situation. Under the new arrangement, my father, a union construction worker (pipe fitter-welder) had more than his hands full. We struggled and survived on our own with Dad and just us kids for the first year and a half to two years after the split with my youngest brother of only one year of age and the fact that there was no adult over thirteen years of age in the household when Dad was at work. The youngest, an infant, was directed by an order of the state to be placed in a foster home, and we only were able to have him with us on weekends. It was during this time that my father was also dealing with some disciplinary issues with my two oldest brothers and decided that he would direct them, at least during the winter months (motorcycle racings off season), to attend the nearby Baptist church on Sundays in an effort to establish some good and orderly direction for them, which he believed they were struggling with and in need of. On the advice of an older fellow worker who was a Christian, he decided church might help.

As a "broken" family, we, or I, have experienced some rather difficult periods. I have never felt as if we had such bad times, for I know many do and some even far worse. There were also, given that, many happy times of familial interaction and love. Praise God. One of these that is strong in my memory is of the many times that either as a whole family or even in smaller groups of just a few of us that we would many times when camping, going hiking, or exploring naturally discuss the possibility of us or others getting lost on their excursions into the *deeper* woods. Always in this discussion would come up the issue of the potential of us getting lost also.

While quite a fearful thought that we were discussing as we were exploring, we wisely thought that we should be aware of and try to leave some form of a marking of our path so that were we to get lost or completely lose our way, we would be able to get back somehow or be able to trace or follow the "markings" to find our way out or to *safety*. Not that we always actually did it. We discussed and visualized the scenarios both ways vividly. Our fear of getting *lost* was well founded, especially since we were familiar with many classical stories or movies that would utilize this as part of the plot in their storyline. Fortunately, in these instances, we (I) never did.

Now, back to our father's effort at some good, orderly direction for me and my siblings. This Baptist church that I am speaking of and its pastor, who was a rather fire and brimstone preacher, as I remem-

THERE IS A DOORWAY...

ber, played an extremely significant part in my evolution as a believer, and he is a critical piece in this crumb trail that I have mentioned that God has led me on. Now there became a time when the Baptist church was holding a membership attendance drive to grow church participation and membership. In this attendance drive, there was a prize table with three prizes for the first three places of church members that brought along the most new guests to the Sunday services.

They were given a card, and every time they brought a guest, who was not a member previously, they would punch their card for as many as they brought to each service. So my oldest brother asked our father for permission to bring his three younger siblings in an effort to try to win the contest at the church. I was one of and the oldest of the three being considered. My father permitted his request as we had not been attending there prior with him thinking for certain it would be good for us and the oldest at the same time, the ole "two birds downed with one stone" so to speak. So over the next several weeks, we attended the Baptist Temple's services and even spent some time going downstairs beneath the sanctuary into the Sunday school classes. Now it was on about the second or third Sunday I attended as a guest "to help my brother" win one of the prizes on the prize table for bringing in the most new attendees that there was a certain part of the Sunday service where the pastor made a request for an altar call.

At this point, I was approximately eleven years old, and my oldest brother was fourteen, who was generally in charge of the rest of us when dad was not present, and apparently, my older brother did not know what an altar call was. So he quickly asked my next older brother, who was two years older than I, at thirteen, "What's an altar call?"

His reply was, as he shrugged, "I don't know."

So in a weird but surprising response to that, the oldest said to me, "Ricky, Ricky, put your hand up!" And I did. The pastor, whom I was slightly afraid of prior to this, came right down the aisle to the pew where we were all sitting, and he reached over and grabbed me gently by the hand, helping me up from my seat as he walked me to the front of the church, opening the gate to the sanctuary, guiding me into a place where we knelt. After laying his hands on me, he prayed over me. The pastor had me repeat after him the sinner's prayer.

Then he gave me a miniature Bible of the New Testament. He also showed me John 3:16, and we read it together, which I memorized instantly, and I have never forgotten. It took many years for me to completely understand the significance of that day's events. For it was not until many years later when I began to glean the significance of that day and the impact and direction it would have on my life. To this day, it still blows my mind of my older brother's actions that morning at that Sunday service where I am going to suggest was a critical and most pivotal point in my life and my walk, as it began to increase my quest and awareness to know God. Jesus Christ entered my heart and mind that day, and I know it. We continued to attend the Baptist church on Sundays, and then we would spend some time in the basement in the Sunday school classrooms after the church's regular service.

There I was taught Old Testament stories and lessons that were worked out on a felt board, with cutouts reenacting the Old Testament teachings. I cannot say I learned all the Old Testament stories, but it was very foundational in establishing some of the pinnacles of the Old Testament, such as Moses, Jonah and the whale, Samson, David and Goliath, etc. Again, it's the most important concept to learning in establishing some understanding of the Old Testament, and to add to that, not only was I getting biblical and historical information for my foundation of Bible knowledge, but by sheer happenstance, or was it? That I also, by the guiding hand of the pastor, was introduced to God and welcomed to and into what was an official starting point to this quest, search, and relationship with Almighty God. God was now on my radar screen.

It was with that copy of the New Testament that miniature little Bible that Pastor Boaman gave me that day that I began to read the scriptures of the New Testament. Over the next several years, I continued to read, especially in times of difficulty and strife. I would read that little Bible about the son of God, the man, Jesus. Eventually, we stopped going to the Baptist church; the oldest two quit going altogether, of course, not until after the oldest won third prize in the attendance drive and received a Polaroid instant camera for the effort.

Dad now started taking the same three little guys, of which I was one of, back to a different Methodist church than before that was only a couple of miles away from our house, which was a bit closer than the one we went to prior to our move. The three of us, minus the older two, attended Methodist youth group on Wednesday nights and Sunday school at that little Methodist church for the next few years. I was even chosen by the Methodist youth group leader Joyce Wright to stand in for the minister on a Sunday when he would be out of town and conducted the whole Sunday service as the pastor, at about fifteen to sixteen years old. I continued to read and study the scriptures; wherever the Good Lord had me, whatever I was enduring, I continued to read. Was I angelic in behavior? Hardly, but God's goodness had taken root in me, and I was definitely a "glass is over half full" type of individual. For it is God's goodness that leads us to repentance, not ours.

Feeling blessed and special to God before I ever really had any understanding of such things, I was continuing to gain Bible knowledge. A little here, and a little there. As a teenager, I had become our church group's president at the Methodist Youth Fellowship of our local church, which met at the instructor's home on Wednesday evenings. As I had mentioned previously, I was fifteen, and our minister at that time, Wayne Grier, went out of town and would be gone for the weekend. So our MYF Bible teacher Mrs. Wright, who by coincidence was also my high school bus driver, questioned me, asking if I could stand in for Pastor Grier while he was away and conduct the Methodist church's Sundays service, which I did.

It was such a momentous event in our family that my father, along with the same two older brothers, attended as well, and Dad got a picture of me preaching that Sunday's sermon, which I had gotten to prepare. It was a huge event for me in my teen years, giving more evidence of how the Lord has sought after me for a very long time. By the time I had turned eighteen, I was preparing to go off for the first year of college; well, actually, the only year. I had developed a specific interest in the reading of and an attempting to understand one of the most prophetic books of the Bible, the book of Revelation, which is positioned at the end of the New Testament. There was something about its placement, as the last book of the

New Testament, and in that specific definition of its title, which I understood to mean "the revealing."

I also had come across, bought, and read the book by Hal Lindsey, *The Late Great Planet Earth*. So in error (or was it?), I jumped over the books penned by Paul and thought, *Heck, let's skip to the end and go straight to the climax!* A monumental error or mistake on my part, in reference to my spiritual development. These prophecy studies captured my focus and imagination at that time, and I remember during my college year spending much of my free time in my apartment reading repeatedly in an attempt to attest the verses to memory, from beginning to end, many times, the last book of the Bible, the Revelation. Maybe as many as fifteen times. It began to be my area of focus over the next many years fruitlessly as I tried to gain some clarity or understanding of this last book of the Bible. As we know, it is most complex, especially to one whom much of the truth has not been revealed yet. One of the by-products of this effort was that I had indelibly impressed the text of the book of Revelation in my memory, after all that repetitive reading and study.

That is the very method that most Bible study is employed, by the repetitive reading and study of the Scripture text, and is affirmed by this, "Consequently, Faith comes by hearing and hearing by the word about Christ," as it says in Romans 10:17. For there is an incredible transition that occurs over the course of a lifetime of study into the Word of God. Reading it is good, but hearing is even better. As I asserted before, "For it is the goodness of God that leads man to repentance." Romans 2:4 says clearly, "Or do you show contempt for the riches of his kindness, forbearance and patience not realizing that God's kindness is intended to lead you to repentance?" It has been through this knowledge that has been revealed, through devoted study, that the clarity of the gospel has been delivered to me by God's word, through the Holy Spirit. Over the last few years, I have consummately been bathing in His Word, daily immersing and washing and staying grounded in the teachings of the scriptures and the leading of the Holy Spirit. Through these efforts, His word has been illuminated and has completely come alive, as He has showered me in His restorative Grace. Praise God.

It has been a continued journey, almost an intimate dance if you would, between me and the Holy Spirit of God. Specifically, since I have kept myself grounded in the study and hearing of His word not as much as I should have previously, but thankfully never straying too far away to not hear the shepherd's voice and stay connected, I had continually sought wisdom and knowledge about the creator and anything that would clarify understanding or help to illuminate the challenge that was in front of me, driven by my intellectual curiosity to understand life and its meaning and purpose to get to know if possible and understand God.

I contemplated and considered other religious disciplines, but to the words of truth that I had already received, nothing compares or could stand up to the knowledge, wisdom, and historicity of the Bible. I continued to search the scriptures, reading in the Old Testament and the New alike, meditating on the word, and studying over time under various Bible teachers, as the likes of Jack Van Impe, Herbert W. Armstrong, Dr. Charles Stanley, Oral Roberts, Rex Humbard, Jimmy Swaggart, John and Joel Osteen, John Hagee, and my Breakthrough pastor and teacher as of the last few years, Singapore's Pastor Joseph Prince, and an Oklahoma rancher and Bible teacher Les Feldick. For how many times that I must have read the scripture that says in Matthew 6:33, "But seek first His kingdom and His righteousness, and all these things will be given to you as well."

It was in Pastor Prince's book *Live the Let Go Life* that the scripture gained the clarity I needed to begin this logjam breakthrough, and it hit me in a way that it never had before, opening my understanding of God's Holy Scriptures and the gospel of Grace that I so much needed. It was as if a fog was being lifted from before me, then driving it home by backing it up with Romans 14:17, which says, "The kingdom of God is not eating and drinking, but righteousness and peace and joy in The Holy Spirit." And *shazam*! Just like that, it was as if the steps of the elusive path to the truth of God's word had become electrically illuminated. The puzzle pieces have so begun to fit and yield incredible clarity of understanding of His word that has now been delivered to me from God in my journey and search. A fire has been lit to the point where this book is my prayer and effort to share these truths and glorify the Father, Son, and Holy Spirit of God and to teach the only real Gospel of Grace and Truth of Jesus Christ and His delivered Peace to all who believe.

This was accomplished through the finished work of the cross, thus paying the price for our redemption and salvation. His summation and conclusion of this redemptive work were effectively wrapped up with Godly authority in Christ's words on the cross, "When he had received the drink, Jesus said, 'It is finished!' With that, He bowed his head and gave up his spirit," as it says in John 19:30.

It was for emphasis that I concluded that last paragraph where and as I did. For short of Christ's second coming that paragraph concludes with the most climactic and important scene of the whole Bible, of which there are many. This event preceded the pivotal event of His resurrection on the third day after His crucifixion. These events are most weighty matters, for our Faith hinges and depends on their very actuality, of which I am most certain. Now there was a good period of my life where some of these questions were open-ended mysteries. But thanks be to the Grace of God for the revelation of key factors that were amiss for one reason or another. Possibly even for the fact that I hadn't arrived at a level of understanding to launch me to the plateau of illumination of these what were previously mysteries, are now revealed.

Through a more accurate understanding and study of the Holy Scriptures, primarily a deeper study in the writings of the apostle Paul, from Romans to Philemon and Hebrews, which delivered much-needed clarity and further understanding of the overall plan of our salvation with God for now and eternity, coupled with my last two-plus years of study under Pastor Joseph Prince and another Bible teacher and cattle rancher from Oklahoma, Les Feldick, many revelations of the word have been received as wisdom and knowledge continue to be revealed.

It is after my lifelong quest for this elusive wisdom and knowledge of enlightenment, through the searching of the Holy Scriptures, that I have clearly discerned this from the leading of the *Spirit of*

Truth into the understanding of His *word*. The Bible contains all truth and is the complete revealed knowledge of God—of this I am most certain. If I had to minimize it to a singularity, I can easily say that the ultimate reality of this existence is Jesus Christ, and I am very aware that that is a most powerful statement. And the text of the Bible bears it out. I have been led by the Holy Spirit and have been taught by His word and leading that two of the most weighty concepts that we are faced with as Christians are the main subjects of condemnation and forgiveness, both concepts to which the gospel of Jesus directly pertains.

Our need for and His plan of our eternal redemption and salvation—these issues are the weightiest of matters and at one time or another will affect all our lives. This topic comes up when considering eternity with God or separation by eternal damnation from Him, which is not what He desires for us. He would want that none should perish. It is His long-suffering and patience that have kept Him holding back until He decides it has come to the fullest and fullness of time. So that many have the chance to come to repentance from sin and be saved—another pertinent concept of any deep thinker or Bible student and one some may never concern themselves with.

There is only one sin in this world that God will not forgive until we repent, which means change your mind. That one sin is this: Unbelief, the denying and rejection of His son, Jesus Christ, the Messiah whom He sent. With belief in Jesus Christ (Yeshua), which means salvation in Hebrew, we are made righteous with God by our belief in His Son whom He sent for our redemption. For by one man's sin, death and iniquity have entered this world (Adam), and by one man's act of *Grace*, all have been offered the provision to receive eternal salvation in our Lord and Savior Jesus Christ.

In Romans 6:23, it states emphatically and most profoundly, "For the wages of sin is death, but the gift of God is eternal life in Christ Jesus our Lord." Sin is bad and will lead your pathway to destruction. While imminently important, it is not the most important revelation of this specific scripture. What is, is what it says next, "The gift of God is eternal life in Christ Jesus our Lord." Not to glaze over this without a closer look, let's examine this statement. If you have to do something to earn a gift, then it is not a gift. But this says, "The gift of God." Now however hard this may be to grasp and believe, a gift is a freely offered blessing, no matter whom it is from. If it is not, then it is not a gift. Not from God, and it is not of His Grace. But it truly is a gift. For we know God cannot lie. For God is completely righteous, pure love and intelligence.

And given that, it says just what it means. Not confession, not baptism, not tithing, not a performance-associated requirement of any kind, other than the requirement of just simply to believe God's Word as truth. Faith in Jesus Christ. Believe and receive. The works we perform are out of our awareness of God's sacrificial love for us, and they are an expression of our love for Him. Works of any kind are not a prerequisite for our eternal salvation, which we have just seen is delivered to us solely by our Faith in God and belief in His Word to us—that is, belief in the Son whom the Father sent.

The repentance that is required is the changing of your mind and perception that we are no longer condemned if we receive the gift of salvation through Jesus Christ our Lord, freely offered by His Grace through our Faith in Him, and the finished work of our redemption that was accomplished on the cross at Calvary. Where everything changed!

Unfortunately, many teach, and erringly so, that if you try to live a good life and be a good person, that maybe, hopefully, one day you may achieve a righteous standing before God. This is heresy. We are made righteous before God, under the *new* dispensation of God's Grace, which removed, replaced, and fulfilled all the Law and the prophets and was instituted forever by Jesus Christ's finished work of the cross.

God in His infinite wisdom, who knows all things and constructed the very space-time continuum within which we exist, had waited to the very fullness of time to a specific point when He delivered the Christ to us for our redemption. Furthermore, He has informed us that He is the *alpha* and the *omega*—Greek translations of what he would have said, "The Aleph and the Tav," Hebrew for the first and last letters of the Hebrew alphabet. He is the beginning and the end. He is in us, we in Him, and He by His power holds the whole universe together until the return of our Lord and Savior Jesus

Christ when we as believers will see Him as we are called up into the air to meet with Him, having been changed at His appearance into our new and resurrected bodies, as it says in 1 Thessalonians 4:14–18:

> For we believe that Jesus died and rose again, and so we believe that God will bring with Jesus those who have fallen asleep in him. According to the Lord's word, we tell you that we who are still alive, who are left until the coming of the Lord, will certainly not precede those who have fallen asleep. For the Lord himself will come down from heaven, with a loud command, with the voice of the Archangel and with the trumpet call of God, and the dead in Christ will rise first. After that, we who are still alive and are left will be caught up together with them in the clouds to meet the Lord in the air. And so we will be with the Lord forever. Therefore encourage one another with these words.

In the very next paragraph in 1 Thessalonians, it lists for us how we are to await His coming, and it is very insightful. In 1 Thessalonians 5:1–10, it says:

> Now, brothers and sisters, about times and dates we do not need to write to you. For, you know very well that the day of the Lord will come like a thief in the night. While people are saying," Peace and safety" destruction will come on them suddenly, as labor pains on a pregnant woman, and they will not escape. But you, brothers and sisters, are not in darkness, so that this day should surprise you like a thief. You are all children of the light and children of the day. We do not belong to the night nor to the darkness. So then, let us

> be awake and sober. For those who sleep, sleep at night, and those who get drunk, get drunk at night. But since we belong to the day, let us be sober, putting on *faith* and love as a breastplate, and the hope of salvation as a helmet. For God did not appoint us to suffer wrath, but to receive salvation through our Lord Jesus Christ. He died for us so that, whether we are awake or asleep, we may live together with him.

Our God is such a magnificent God, and there is no other, providing us so completely His complete story. His story. History. There is so much wisdom, knowledge, and powerful revelation in our Father's word. He has revealed Himself to us through His word the Holy Bible. In the opening paragraph, from John 1, we were establishing the fact that Jesus Christ is the Word. As we know in Bible study, we back everything up from His Word, the Bible, fully His Word from cover to cover; it is both a literal and pictorial message to us that reveals the intimate message of our loving Father as He reveals His love for us, His immense desire for a human family, and the story of the gospel of Grace and Peace and Truth in the life and sacrifice of His only Son, our Lord and Savior Jesus Christ, the prophesied Messiah.

Certainly, the pivotal plank in my platform of understanding was firmly put into place after receiving the Teaching of the Gospel of Grace and Truth from Pastor Joseph Prince. Not that other ministers were not preaching and revealing this monumental truth of God and His word but promoting it through the teaching that we are to look to Jesus and His righteousness and not focusing on our own performance to achieve ours but that we are made the righteousness of God by our belief in our Lord and Savior Jesus Christ and the finished work of the cross. *Bam!* For as it says in Romans 3:21–26:

> But now apart from the Law. The righteousness of God has been made known, to which the Law and the prophets testify. This righteousness

is given through Faith in Jesus Christ to all who believe. There is no difference between Jew or Gentile, for all have sinned and fall far short of the glory of God, and all are justified freely by His *grace* through the redemption that came by Christ Jesus. God presented Christ as a sacrifice of atonement, through the shedding of his blood—to be received by Faith. He did this to demonstrate his righteousness, because in his forbearance he had left the sins committed beforehand unpunished-he did it to demonstrate his righteousness at the present time, so-as-to-be just, and the one who justifies those who have Faith in Jesus.

So this amazing God and our Lord and Savior Jesus Christ took on all sin and became poor so that we who believe could become rich in Him. It is what is referred to as the divine exchange. Jesus Christ, our Savior and Redeemer, took on a debt He did not owe so we could receive blessings and honor that we have not earned. Amen. Thanks be to our God.

So I can say experientially that for me, until I began to grasp the Law of Grace and its conceptual application and I stopped focusing on my performance, as required by the demands of the Law of Moses, which unfortunately is still being taught erroneously in some modern churches today. I realized before having these truths revealed through His word, along with the opening of my mind by the leading of the Holy Spirit that I had literally hit a wall of confusion that had me mentally, spiritually, and literally chasing my own tail.

But Praise God, the Father, and His Son and our Lord and Savior Christ Jesus and His Holy Spirit that He also made me aware that He was looking for me and had been calling for quite some time. For we cannot seek our own righteousness, for without Christ in us, we have none. For our salvation is not earned, having been misled to believe that we can earn it or even attempt to. In Romans 6:23, it says, "For the wages of sin is death, but the gift of God is eternal life in Christ Jesus our Lord." Our eyes and mind are to be on our Savior, Jesus Christ, for it is His act that performs and accomplishes our salvation.

We are justified by our *faith* and belief in Him. That is where our sanctification occurs. It is totally by His Grace that the new covenant has been and is established as a free gift for the taking. Sin is never the obstacle. It is the lack of *faith*. In Mark 2:2–5, it says:

> They gathered in such large numbers that there was no room left, not even outside the *door*, and he preached the word to them. Some men came, bringing to him a paralyzed man, carried by four of them. Since they could not get him to Jesus because of the crowd, they made an opening in the roof above Jesus by digging through it and lowered the mat the man was lying on. When Jesus saw their *faith*, he said to the paralyzed man, "Son, your sins are forgiven."

Like the paralyzed man, once I was able to see the lack of understanding in this very area was where and why I had hit a so-called ceiling that was blocking a fuller understanding and, essentially for me, the missing link or the missing building block that was essential and imperative for me to grow further in wisdom, true knowledge, and a much firmer grasp on a full understanding of the gospel and Faith in and on Jesus Christ. By the paralyzed man's and his friends' actions, their Faith in Jesus's ability to heal was most evident. It is much similar for us today—words are fine and serve, but it is with our actions that we will bear out our love and acceptance of His Grace poured out upon us. Again, it says in Romans 10:17–18:

> Consequently, *faith* comes from hearing the message, and the message is heard through the word about Christ. "But I ask; Did they hear not? Of course they did."

So thankfully here I would like to state, I am one of the fortunate and blessed individuals that the Lord and Holy Spirit of God have chosen to reveal these truths of the Gospel of Grace and Peace that is given to us from the Father by His Son Jesus Christ and the finished work of the cross and me believing His word is true. By understanding more clearly His Grace, it has unchained my Faith, and this wayward "prodigal son" heard the shepherd's voice and knew it was time to come back home to receive the love from the Father.

It was in the revelations of God through His word and my study over the years that revealed the rareness and specialty of purpose and selection I feel and have felt since I began to be aware of a calling to share His *word*, His Gospel, wisdom and knowledge and love the Father has for us through His Son. For in almost every direction of the reality we all share, there is no more consequential information availed to us in this existence. For many people share a saying, "Life, we are not going to get out of here alive."

Well, I would unequivocally suggest that that is inherently not true. For the result of what this wonderful Gospel of Grace and Peace delivers to us is eternity with God in heaven! Which to me is an exceedingly great reward and bonus to the love, presence, and protection that I already now feel, share, and rest in. Amen. Praise be to God the Father, Son, and Holy Spirit. Praise be to the Most High God; there is no other.

Yes, praise be to our Lord and Savior Jesus Christ. In Colossians 2:9–10, it says:

> For in Christ, all the fullness of the deity lives in bodily form, and in Christ, you have been brought to fullness. He is the head over every power and authority.

To add to this and to clarify with even more specificity, it says just above that in Colossians 2:8–9:

> See to it that no one takes you captive through hollow and deceptive philosophy, which

> depends on human tradition and elemental spiritual forces of this world rather than on Christ.

Potent words and a compelling suggestion that I have taken to heart and mind literally and firmly kept my eyes and mind fixed on the prize—our Lord Jesus Christ!

Very straightforward now, as I stand here on what has been revealed in the knowledge of His *word*, I have struggled equally in life and understanding over the years on the way to what I can only describe as illumination and enlightenment. Obviously, there are many paths to this specific revelation or destination of the knowledge of God. But I must be clear, there is only one conclusion. Referring back to Colossians 1:15–20:

> The Son is the image of the invisible God, the firstborn over all creation. In him all things were created: things in heaven and on earth, visible and invisible, whether thrones or powers or rulers or authorities; all things were created through Him and for Him. He is before all things, and in Him all things are held together. And He is the head of the body, the church, He is the beginning and the firstborn from among the dead. So that in everything He might have supremacy. For God was pleased to have all his fullness dwell in Him, and through Him to reconcile to Himself all things, whether things on earth, or things in heaven, by making peace through His blood, shed on the cross.

Praise the Most High God. Praise Jesus. Praise the Lord. Thanks be to the Holy Spirit.

Today is election day, November 3, 2020. It is a time of much contention in this country that we live in. The election will be between the current president and Joe Biden, and by all that is holy to the Lord's, I pray His will prevails. As I judge a man, the race is not even close. We are in the midst presently of the COVID-19 pandemic. The current caseload is increasing, and deaths are on the rise again as we head into the winter in this fall of 2020.

Much of the future of this country, the United States of America, stands in the balance on the outcome of this election. But I fear not either way, for I know that the good Lord Almighty is in control. He is the Alpha and the Omega, the Aleph and the Taph. He is the beginning and the end. In Him, all things exist and all things are held together, and therein, I fear not. In 365 places in the Holy Bible, our God has used the words or the phrase, "Fear not," "Do not be afraid," and "Have no fear" or another very similar or slightly variant version of the phrase. One for every day of the year, which I believe was not a coincidence.

As I have learned through Bible study and have confirmed that as believers in the Lord's word, that we are in the world, but we are not of the world. As we have been sanctified, set apart as believers, in our savior and deliverer, the Lord Jesus Christ, the holy one of Israel, the Messiah. In 1 John 4:4, it affirms this where it says, "You, dear children, are from God, and have overcome them, because the one who is in you is greater than the one who is in the world."

Today is November 17, 2020. The election has been over now a full two weeks, between Joe Biden and the sitting president, Donald Trump, who has yet to concede his loss or defeat in the election to Joe Biden by over five million votes and by a loss of the same margin in the electoral college that he won by four years ago. Since this is a book on Truth and the Grace of Jesus Christ, I cannot help but insert the time frame and the events that are going on in the world as I am writing this book.

We are in a most uncertain time for the sitting president. Mr. Trump has failed to recognize the outcome of the election by some delusion that there was systemic cheating. Whereas every court case that his lawyers have filed has lost or has been thrown out, discredited, and has not gained any traction whatsoever in any of the states. To this time, there is only a recount in the states where the margin was so close that by law, that it was required to have those.

However, unequivocally, there have been no cases of wrongdoing in illegal voting in any of the states where it was challenged. In fact, the one story that I saw that had been portrayed on the news as voter fraud spoken of just above, supposedly a dead voter, was clarified when they found out it was the voter's widow voting in the name of her husband as she always had her whole life since he had passed. I, as a citizen and a patriot to these United States and not to either party, write of these concerns that I have because we are in a most unstable period. I have many legitimate concerns, which I will not go into detail about here. I only pray that the good Lord's will, will be upon all things, and my fears will be allayed, and a smooth transition will happen from the forty-fifth to the forty-sixth president-elect, Joe Biden. No leader can be a panacea or a cure-all for the world's ills. We look to the Lord Jesus Christ to solve and bring peace to the earth ultimately. But in the stead, till then, I pray and feel that the election of Joe Biden will protect this country and undo things that have made us more vulnerable over the last four years and have moved us dangerously closer toward fascism, further exposing the United States internally and externally.

One of the *gifts* that has been imputed to me as evidenced by my years of interest and study is in the field of Bible prophecy. It is one of my driving factors, given the knowledge I have gained and zeal for such a complex topic. That dive will likely need to be for the next or another book. However, it is the revelation of the end times that I have been exposed to, affected by, and much more reverent of God for the big picture or rather His plan for our future, immediate, and further out. The effort or purpose of this work has been to transfer information that I have gleaned from my study of the Holy Scriptures that point, affirm, and confirm the reason for and the meaning of life.

The establishment of just who God is and evidence the very character and condition of His heart, His love for us, and why we are even here—these are mysteries that man has been searching to unlock to discover the truth. That is just exactly what we have here. I will go out on a limb here and state unequivocally—sustained by the complete book, the Bible, cover to cover of the Holy Scriptures, old and new alike—that Jesus Christ is Lord and is, in two words, completely the *ultimate reality*.

All things are created by Him, for Him, and through Him. In Him, all things are held together. Just as it says in 1 Corinthians 8:6.

The remaining part of this chapter will be an effort to establish that very concept to develop it even further and back it with scripture the deity of Jesus Christ, as well as supporting it by the other chapters of this book. For God the Father, God the Son, and God the Holy Spirit are God—one God with three distinct personalities, roles, or similitudes within which revealed God's very nature and desire for a familial relationship with us.

The following are two scripture verses or rather a small paragraph from two of the books of the New Testament that in my opinion, and of many others, will support and, more than that, even verify in God's word, His very purpose. This one is a continuation of verses first speaking of John the Baptist and then Jesus from John 1 that I used earlier for its profoundness, it addresses the spiritual economy that we exist in. As it says in John 1:8–18:

> He himself was not the light; he came only as a witness to the light. The true light that gives light to everyone was coming into the world. He was in the world, and the world was made through Him, the world did not recognize Him. He came to that which was His own, but His own did not receive Him. Yet to all who did receive him, to those who believed in his name, He gave the right to become children of God—children born not of natural descent, nor of human decision or a husband's will, but born of God. The Word became flesh and made his dwelling among us. We have seen his glory, the glory of the one and only son, who came from the Father, full of Grace and Truth. John testified concerning him. He cried out, saying," this is the one I spoke about when I said, "He who comes after me has surpassed me, because he was before me." Out of his fullness we have all received *grace* in place of *grace* already given. For the Law was given through Moses; Grace and truth came

through Jesus Christ. No one has ever seen God, but the one and only son, who is himself God, and is in closest relationship with the Father, has made him known.

The next scripture that I will reference will drive this concept home even further. If there is any uncertainty or lack of clarity, as I had stated above, the verses begin in John, verse 8, speaking of John the Baptist, who is to come just before Christ to announce His coming. Verse 9, 10, 11, and 12 speak of Christ, and notably, verse 11 speaks of the Hebrew or Israelite people when it speaks to that "he came to that which was his own, but his own did not receive him." Verse 12 speaks of us when it says, "Yet to all who did receive him, (the Gentiles), also the believing Jews, all those who believed in his name, he gave the right to become children of God," and 13 continues, "Children born not of natural descent nor of human decision, or a husband's will, but born of God." To further emphasize the power of Almighty God that was in His Son Jesus Christ, we will look at 2 Corinthians 3:15–18:

> Even to this day, when Moses is read, a veil covers their hearts. But whenever anyone turns to the Lord, the veil is taken away. now, the Lord is the spirit, and where the Spirit of the Lord is, there is freedom. And we all, who with unveiled faces contemplate the Lord's glory, are being transformed into his image with ever increasing glory, which comes from the Lord, who is the spirit.

Now this is a reference, I believe, to the veil that blocks our receiving and understanding of Grace that is emitted today as one attempts to uphold the Ten Commandments of Moses's Law and thus establish their own righteousness by performing or upholding the old Mosaic Law. This is an extremely deep and pivotal concept that can be borne out much further here. For it was pivotal in my transcending the confusion of legalistic beliefs, or the Law, which just refers to the remnants of the Ten Commandments being mixed in with Jesus's law of Grace and Truth and how it basically undermines and takes the power away from the full and true gospel of Jesus Christ of the Grace and Truth and Peace. For that economy referred to under the Mosaic Law or the Law of Moses (referring to the keeping of the Ten Commandments) was the cornerstone of the first covenant, between the people of Israel and Jehovah God. Effectively, the Messiah Jesus Christ and the work that was accomplished at the cross on which our salvation, justification, and redemption all rest did just exactly that. It was the fulfillment and the ultimate sacrifice, providing the blood of the Messiah, which once and for all removes the need for the blood of sacrificial animals.

One single drop of the holy blood that was shed from the God and man Jesus Christ, the Messiah, sent from the Father was all that was necessary to remove all sin and wickedness from the world, providing our atonement. It was a vast overpayment! And as He said by His own words that He and the Father are one and of which the Jewish people at that time were ready to stone Him for saying; however, He could not help that, for only the truth was in Him. For as it says, also in the word, "Jesus Christ is the way the truth and the light." A most interesting insight here comes in the book of Hebrews 10. Paul writes and quotes words of Christ revealed to him during the revelations given after his road to Damascus transformation in the time that Paul spent with the Holy Spirit once he became a believer in Jesus Christ.

> The Law is only a shadow of the good things that are coming—not the realities themselves. For this reason, it can never, by the same sacrifices repeated endlessly year after year, make perfect those who draw near to worship. Otherwise, would they not have stopped being offered? For the worshipers would have been cleansed once for all, they would no longer have felt guilty for their sins. But those sacrifices were an annual reminder

of sins. It is impossible for the blood of bulls and goats to take away sins. Therefore, when Christ came into the world, he said: "Sacrifice and offering you did not desire, but a body you prepared for me; With burnt offerings and sin offerings, you were not pleased. Then I said, 'Here I am—it is written about me in the scroll—I have come to do your will, my God'." First, he said, "Sacrifices and burnt offerings and sin offerings you did not desire, nor were you pleased with them"—though they were offered in accordance with the Law. Then he said, "Here I am, I have come to do your will." He sets aside the first to establish the second. And by that will, we have been made Holy through the sacrifice of the body of Jesus Christ once for all.

So then, in case you did not catch that, and apparently, this is where many doctrinal errors are made, it clearly says that God sets aside the first, being the old covenant, the Mosaic Law, which is performance-based and legalist in concept, demanding complete obedience to all ten of the commandments, which falsely suggested and attempted to establish a false righteousness or a self-righteousness, not yielding to the new covenant teaching, which has been established through Jesus Christ, the Messiah. Our justification by Faith to the one true gospel, given through the finished work on the cross where He shed His blood by Grace to all who believe.

Over the last two and a half years, my situation availed itself to where I was able to immerse completely in the study of God's Word. One of the key concepts that has been evidenced and is most effective is the continual bathing daily in His word, the scriptures. For the more that I have studied, the more His living word has come alive. One of the blessings that I have noticed over the years that I have tried to gain an understanding of God and His plan is that the many years that I studied, even though it seemed to have taken me so long to get to a competent level of understanding, which had eluded me for a long time, that I continued to gain foundational knowledge, acquiring wisdom, and that the search was not in vain or fruitless. It all continued to feed toward the compilation of knowledge until I was able to reach a critical point in correct understanding and reached a certain "saturation level" to get to where the Holy Spirit gave me clarity in the study of the word that has removed my "veil" thereof. This veil or blocking to godly truth and knowledge is emitted from our foolish and erred belief that we can earn or achieve our salvation and that distances us from God. When it is clearly the free gift of God offered to us all by His Grace to all who will *believe* in God, His Word, and our Lord and Savior Jesus Christ. Faith plus nothing.

Now, one of the most problematic pieces to my own puzzle that was missing from the puzzle box I was working with, metaphorically. That was contributed to by the fact that I had not previously diligently searched and continued to read and study at the propensity that I now was with my progression of the New Testament, where I had previously stalled in my reading, learning, and studying of the words of the disciples, somewhere in the area of Romans or Acts, at around seventeen years old. I stated before that I had skipped and jumped directly to the book of Revelation at eighteen and totally missing the very powerful gospels of Paul, the whole of the Pauline writings, as it were, which is approximately one-third of the *new covenant.*

It is now that I can see most clearly, especially given the fact that I have learned and studied the writings of Paul and all the Pauline epistles and had picked up where I had left off in my progression of learning scripture at around seventeen, likely not the wisest thing I have ever done. For me, like probably many others, I started driving and being interested in girls, motorcycles, and all the other things that life throws toward us, where we have the impression, at that time, that they are important, and sometimes we don't find out till much later that likely they were not. For it has been over these last two and a half years that by picking up where I had left off and finishing the reading of the epistles of Paul that I had robbed myself of by not staying the course and reading on through Acts, Romans, and on through the rest of Paul's, Peter's, and John's writings and scriptures. Had I not gotten so eager, I wouldn't have jumped over to get to the intrigue of the end.

So my point here is that by foolishly doing so, I omitted one-third of the writings teachings and truth of the New Testament, and upon this reexamination, it is clear to see why true illumination had eluded me for so long, for I don't think you can leave out one-third of the New Testament, or Covenant as I like to assert, especially the Pauline writings, and arrive at the understanding that has now so clearly revealed itself through the Holy Scriptures of God Almighty to me, now diligently seeking the truth. Nonetheless, whatever my dalliances were, I am ever so grateful to the good Father, His Holy Son, and our Holy Spirit, God.

Yes, I am very thankful to God that however I have meandered, whatever the cause, the purpose or reasons for my prolonged search, I am elated at where He has brought my understanding—to the level that I now have. Praise God. Before my revelation of the of His word, the big picture, or God's plan of human salvation that He has installed was not complete nor was I in possession of a coherent and consistent overview of His complete word to us and God's divine plan for our collective future with Him for those who believe. That I am now in possession of. Thanks be to God in the name of Jesus Christ.

One thing that I would like to add here is that through this journey of finding God's answers to the mysteries of this universe, the reasons why we are here, and the knowledge of His love and His blessings, I have become most aware that it is completely instrumental to this enterprise of understanding the reality of God Almighty that we embrace and, yes, be thankful for the challenges and the tribulations, the turmoil, and the strife in this life as well as the blessings for it is during the time of our challenges and our trials where we grow the most and where our metal is hardened, and praise be to God for that.

In a couple of months, I will turn sixty years of age. It is within this composition that I am endeavoring to share the zeal that now consumes me. I now have been able to receive the answers that I was seeking on my lifelong search for the reason for our existence and the knowledge of God through the Holy Bible. I have sized up His word as He has revealed it to us through the Holy Scriptures, and I have found it to be the most solid, accurate, and truthful information that is available anywhere in this universe. God completely encapsulates every facet, reason, and explanation of all His purposes and eventualities.

Jehovah (Yahweh), or God, reveals it all in His life manual to us—the Holy Bible. For just as when you buy a new vehicle, a brand-new vehicle, and you have the intentions of having an experience over many years with this new vehicle, it is important for them to give you the operator's manual to help you navigate and better enjoy your experience. I assert here in this very same way that is exactly what God's Word, the Holy Bible, is for us—an operator's manual for our lives. Those that choose to ignore, discount, or minimize the value, gravity, and ultimate importance of these matters are doing so at their own folly.

Proverbs 9:10 is a scripture that is ultra-foundational, and we will examine the expanse and meaning of its application, as it was first taught to me when I was in my thirties and had met a Jehovah's Witness on this journey of mine for enlightenment. I took up fellowship with him for a year or so and did attend with them at their church, even holding Bible study on Wednesday evenings with my wife and I with the Jehovah's Witnesses "sponsor" that was field working us as new recruits. Doctrinally, I learned that God's name to the Hebrews was Yahweh or YHWH or translated over to English with vowels added as Jehovah.

I found their dedication impressive, and gaining God's revealed name from studying with them and many other solid teachings were gleaned from the experience overall. But once Jesus has claimed you and you have willingly received Him, there is a scripture that Jesus said, "My sheep know my voice, for another they will not follow." And, my friends, I must admit that is exactly what occurred for me. As it became quite apparent that that affiliation was not emanating a clear voice of the shepherd there, as the further that we were involved, it became apparent the group was not for us.

Now getting back to Proverbs 9:10, which I learned along with other integral Bible concepts in my studies with them, and thankfully, again there was not too much rewiring of concepts to be done. Proverbs 9:10–11 says:

> The fear of the LORD is the beginning of wisdom, and knowledge of the Holy One is understanding. For through wisdom, your days will be many, years will be added to your life. If you are wise, your wisdom will reward you, if you are a mocker, you alone will suffer.

Where it says, "The fear of the Lord is the beginning of wisdom," that always came with a sense of and trepidation and intimidation. I had always reasoned that it would likely be interpreted to reverence of the Lord or to be revering of the Lord.

This may well be one of the aspects of the concept of fear referenced here. However, conceptually, what has revealed itself over much closer scrutiny is the fact that our great God in His infinite wisdom uses the term *fear* and interchanges it intermittently as necessary with the word *worship*. Strangely then, where this scripture sets off on the path of intimidation, as I had stated before, God sees this fear or reverence of His great being as a form of worship, of which I found to be the most novel and interesting and making much sense. Even more clearly then, in Hebrew, the word *worship* means "to kiss." How great our mighty God is to devise our reality where our worship of Him is received as a loving kiss to the Father from us, His believing children. For as much as you *believe* is as much as it is.

Chapter 2

Milk and Honey First

This chapter's purpose is to contribute to a baseline of understanding—to add to or to take off from what point in the learning of theology that you are. Starting with an entry-level perspective of the gospel, the Holy Bible, and the gospel story of Christ, the prophecies of His coming, His life, and His death, burial, and resurrection of Jesus, the Messiah. The whole Bible, the Old Testament and the New, from cover to cover, is Jesus Christ in print, about Him, Him and the Father, His Words and Him typified in print, His Holy Spirit, and the documenting of His patience with the chosen people, Israel, through whom would come the Messiah.

It is necessary for the course of this work to highlight, pick, and choose and to steer or direct the purpose of this undertaking to what I have been led by the Holy Spirit to share, point out, or draw your attention to where these answers are for the knowledge and clarity of all truth and wisdom that I have received by the Holy Spirit's direction through the Word. For the Bible is a large knowledge-and-information-packed "treasure chest." It says in John 14:26, "The Holy Spirit will teach us all things," and that is truly where my wisdom, insight, and direction have come. The choice I have made to write of these things of God, the true gospel, and of the Grace and Truth of Jesus Christ has been driven by an inner calling to glorify the Father, through Jesus Christ's Words and works, and to establish and teach this Gospel of Grace and Truth of Jesus Christ. This is a calling that has been on me since I was a youngster, and has been well explained to us, mightily and primarily, in the writings of Paul in the New Testament gospels.

This information has knocked down the roadblocks that were impeding my understanding. It is for these reasons that I am moved from within to share the truth of these findings that can be and are found in God's Word, the Holy Bible. To help render a clearer understanding or undo some of the false teachings that have crept into many churches and possibly even reignite or to fire up a passion or calling for you to read your Bible to learn and understand further. That would be hitting the bull's-eye that I have targeted to glorify the Father, Jehovah (Yahweh), and the Word of God, Jesus Christ (Son, Yeshua), and the Holy Spirit.

In my early years of study into the New Testament, I developed a strong attraction in the study of the Bible prophecy. While in my year of college, I endeavored to understand the book of Revelation, possibly more clearly by reading it over and over again, at least to a minimum of fifteen times. I have continued over the many years since in reading and learning and continuing to cultivate my understanding in the area of prophecy. It has been with many new revelations over the last two and a half years in my study of the Bible that I was led to, or rather that I had been shared, the knowledge from the Holy Spirit, and through good teaching, sound doctrine, and diligent study, I have continued bathing in His Word. For all these specific reasons, I do feel a sense of urgency or at least significant importance that has emerged from within and without to share these revelations and this knowledge revealed by the Holy Spirit through the Scriptures during this most intense study.

One of the several impeding factors in my walk with the Lord and searching of the Scriptures for understanding was initially a lack of fuller understanding and a broader vocabulary in the terms used in the discussion of church doctrine and in the Scriptures. For this reason, I have assembled a collection of words and phrases which would lead to a fuller understanding of the Scriptures that had eluded me. Some of that impedance that I speak of was due to some inaccurate doctrine, wrong teaching, as well as a lack of familiarity or understanding of some of the major terms and concepts of the Holy Scriptures. So for those very reasons I am going to do a rather moderate dive to deliver some definitions and expound on some concepts to help broaden your understanding of the gospel message, major concepts, and the words of Scripture. These definitions are to enhance your understanding and to be used as a reference to deliver assistance in this book or in any Bible discussion of these or any related topics. I am certain they will be insightful and add to your fuller understanding.

Glossary

Aaron. Moses's brother, spokesman, high priest, and head of the hereditary priesthood, died at 123 years of age, was mourned thirty days.

Abel. Cain's brother whom he slew.

Ark. a chest, a vessel to float, or both.

Ark of the covenant. or of the testimony or chest of the covenant. The chest containing the tablets of the Law, resting in the tabernacle or in the temple as the Lord instructed Moses.

Adonai. Hebrew for *name of God* or *my Lord*.

Adam. first human son of God, means blood man or mankind.

Advent. Jesus Christ's visit to the earth.

Advocate. supporter, backer, helper (Greek "Paraclete").

Alleluia (Hallelujah). praise ye Jehovah.

Angel. messenger.

Antichrist. against or instead of Jesus Christ.

Annoint. Messiah (Hebrew) and Christ (Greek) means anointed one, three types for bathing, as a sign of respect, and burial, and for shields, sacred things, and people.

Apostle. one sent forth, a messenger with a special commission.

Armageddon. the name given to the final battle between Jesus Christ and Satan and his worldly followers where Jesus Christ will destroy all the enemies of God with the breath of His mouth.

Armor. battle-ready warfare gear, helmet of salvation, breastplate of righteousness, belt of Truth, shield of Faith, the sword of the Spirit, which is God's Word, and shoes, which are ready to bring the "*Good News*" of Peace.

Tower of Babel. an event that occurred in Genesis where the people had gotten together to build a tower to reach God in the heavens, which angered God, causing Him to disperse the people around the earth and to change their languages.

Banquet. feast term used in parable by Christ, as in birthdays, marriages, and funerals.

Baptism. ceremonial rite of purification by water or Holy Spirit, a dedication of one's new life to Christ.

Beatitudes. blessedness, qualities disciples should possess.

Benjamin. son of my right hand or son of strength.

Benomi. son of my sorrow.

Beth. Hebrew for *house*.

Bethel. house of God.

Bethesda. house of Grace.

Bethlehem. house of bread, Jesus was born there, the bread of life.

Berith. covenant.

Britain. covenant people.

Birthright. firstborn claim in succession, if patriarch dies.

Blessing. every good gift from the Father or others.

Blasphemy. to speak lightly or carelessly of God.

Branch. refers in the New Testament to the Messiah and His prospering.

Brimstone. sulfur, destruction.

Burning bush. a thorny bush Moses saw, all-burning and not being consumed, from which Jehovah spoke.

Cain. first son of Adam and Eve; he slew Abel.

Calvary. skull, description of and name of a hill where Jesus was crucified, Golgotha.

Chastisement. discipline, also the plan of God to provide a substitute to bear our sins.

Cherubim. angels, heavenly beings which carry out the tasks of God.

Christ. Messiah or anointed one.

Church. a congregation, Ecclesiastica.

Circumcision. a ceremonial rite of Israel and the Hebrew religion removing of the foreskin.

Contrition. remorse or guilt.
Convocation. a festival where no work can be done.
Cross. symbol of the crucifixion and the rising of Jesus on the third day, conquering over death and sin, the very symbol of the power of our Gospel.
Curse. the reverse of bless.
Damnation. eternal separation from God.
Daniel. major prophet of the Old Testament; means God is my judge.
David. King David who wrote the Psalms; means beloved in Hebrew or chieftain.
Day of the Lord. the beginning of Jesus Christ's second coming.
Deacon. Servant.
Dead Sea scrolls. jars of scrolls found in 1948 in the Dead Sea caves in the Middle East, circa AD 100, confirming the accuracy of the Scriptures.
Disciple. a learner.
Dispensation. a distribution or administrative system.
Dispensation (New). God's plan of salvation for us since Jesus Christ finished work at the cross.
Dispensation (Old). God's plan for the Hebrew people through the Mosaic law.
Divination. foreseeing or telling the future or learning hidden knowledge.
Door. the word used many times referring to opportunity and Christ and freedom and power.
Eden. the garden where Adam and Eve were placed, paradise.
Edify. to build up positively.
Eli. my God.
Elijah. Jehovah is God.
Elisha. God is salvation or God saves.
Elizabeth. God is my oath or house.
Elohim. plural word for God encompasses all three personalities.
El Shaddai. Almighty God.
Emmanuelle. God who is with us.
Enoch. Cain's eldest son. A son of Jared, descendant of Seth.

Epistle. Letters.

Eschatology. systematic theology dealing with doctrine of last things, death, days, and Christ's second coming.

Eve. first woman in the garden of Eden with Adam, taken from Adam's side.

Exodus. second book of the Bible, tells of the Hebrews' journey from slavery in Egypt.

El-Elyon. Most High God.

Faith. *belief* in, trust in the person of Jesus Christ and His redemptive work at Calvary; *Faith* in Jesus Christ alone saves man.

Feed. symbolic as well as literal feed on the bread of life, which is God's Word.

Fellowship. sharing God's Word with believers.

Flesh. a symbol of our sinful nature, reflects also worldly trappings.

Flood. the deluge God used to remove evil and wickedness from the earth, leaving only Noah and seven others saved by the ark to repopulate the world over the last six thousand years.

Free. with no charge or any obligation or requirement of any kind to receive said gift.

Gabriel. man of God, an angel who gave the messages to Mary and Elizabeth.

Genesis. the first book of the Old Testament; the origin or beginning.

Gentiles. all people who were not Israelites.

Ghost. Holy Ghost, equivalent to Holy Spirit.

Gift. a material token or an act proffered with no charge or requirement or obligation.

God. Father, Son, Holy Spirit is God; Jehovah, Yeshua or (Joshua), and the Holy Spirit.

Gospel. the God spell, the good news or truth.

Grace. kindness of God to man. Our God displays His love for us, Grace is not just a dinner blessing. His undeserved kindness to us or His mercies upon us; the dispensation we are presently under since its establishment when Jesus Christ rose on the third day and appeared to the apostles. Most underdeveloped concept of Christianity today. The Law of His Grace and Peace is "By Grace we are saved through our Faith."

Giants. Nephilim or Rapha in Hebrew.
Glory. concerning God; it is the display of His divine attributes and perfection, the Shekinah glory of God housed in the Old Testament in the tabernacle or the ark; His divine presence and handiwork.
Godliness. holiness.
Hallelujah (Alleluia). praise Ye Jehovah.
Hallow. to render or treat as holy.
Hanan. gracious.
Haniel. Grace of God, favor of God.
Hannah. Grace or favor.
Harvest. Bible term when not referring to agriculture, speaking of the gathering of the saints (sanctified believers in Jesus Christ) at the end of this age or crops taken in at the end of the growing season
Heaven. the abode of God, our future existence with God.
Holiness. godliness, separateness.
Holy Spirit. the helper or advocate who teaches us all things; the third figure of the Triune Godhead—God.
History. His story.
High priest. under the old dispensation of the Mosaic Law, the head of the Levitical priesthood; under the New, Jesus Christ is our High Priest.
Herod. Jewish king at the time of Jesus's birth.
Hebrews. designation of Abraham and his descendants by God.
Hell. Hades, a place of retribution for unredeemed man, eternal damnation.
Hesed. Hebrew for mercy.
Honey. the standard of comparison for pleasant things.
Hope. a confident expectation of things prayed for, a gift of the Holy Spirit, trust, confidence, and *faith* and refuge in God.
Hosanna. come Messiah to save us.
Hosea. it means salvation.
Idolatry. worship of foreign idols.
Image of the God. man is made in God's image, body, soul, and spirit, as God is Father, Son, and Holy Spirit.

Immortality. self-conscious continuous state of body, soul, and spirit for eternity.
Immutable. the perfection of God, which is devoid of change.
Impute. to attribute something to a person, to reckon something to the account of another.
Incarnation. John 1:1, "The word became flesh and dwelt among them," the visible appearance of God in human affairs.
Inspiration. special influence of the Holy Spirit to speak or write what God wants to be communicated to others.
Iphadeiaih. Jehovah redeems.
Irijah. Jehovah sees.
Irpeel. God heals.
Isaac. one who laughs, Abraham's son.
Isaiah. Old Testament prophet; it means "salvation of Jehovah."
Ishmael. God hears; Abraham's son by the Egyptian maid Hagar.
Israel. to strive with God; God's chosen, the person and the tribes, the people.
Jacob. son of Isaac and Rebekah, becomes Israel.
James. one of the twelve original apostles, brother of John; there were two James, James the apostle and James Jesus's brother, means to supplant.
Jehoshaphat. Jehovah is judge.
Jehoshuah. Jehovah saves.
Jehovah. the name of God revealed to the Hebrews in the Old Testament, derived from the tetragrammaton YHWH.
Jehozadek. Jah is righteous.
Jeremiah. Jehovah exalts or founds.
Jerusalem. the holy royal city, the only city God has established among men.
Jew. short for members of the tribe of Judah; the two tribes of the southern kingdom, later became to mean all Hebrews.
Joel. Jehovah is God.
Johanan. Jehovah has been *gracious*.
Jonah. means "dove," minor prophet of the Old Testament sent to Nineveh but refused to go, swallowed by a large fish or whale,

and was carried inside for three days, ultimately arriving at Nineveh anyway.

Jeshua. Jehovah is salvation.

Jesus. Yeshua, Messiah, the son of God, the Holy Spirit after Pentecost, God incarnate.

Kolaiah. the voice of Jehovah.

KJV. King James Version of the Bible translated in 1611.

Know. to be well informed about, sure, certain.

Known. of know.

Knowledge. the act, the fact, or state of knowing; enlightenment.

Knowledgeable. of having or showing knowledge or intelligence.

Law. Ten Commandments given to Moses; purpose was to prepare the way for Jesus Christ and shows man's sinful nature, stirs up and demands perfect love for God and neighbor.

Latter. near the end of time, as in the latter days.

Laying of hands. a gift of God of divine healing through Christ or to convey a birthright.

Lamb. symbol for Jesus Christ, the Messiah, the Lamb of God, also relative to us as His young, unlearned sheep.

Lamb of God. Jesus was called that by John the Baptist in Scripture.

Lamech. first poet, Noah's father.

Lamp. a candle or lantern, metaphor for God's way or word, "a lamp unto my feet."

Latin. the language of the Romans, known mostly by the elites.

Lord. term applied to man and God; expresses honor, dignity, and majesty.

Lord's Prayer. a pattern prayer given by example by Jesus as He prayed to the Father.

Lord's Supper. the holy sacraments of bread and wine done by request in remembrance of Christ and the upper room's Last Supper.

Love. the very heart of God as exposed to us by Jesus Christ.

Lucifer. Satan, the devil, adversary, deceiver.

Man, Son of. Jesus Christ.

Man of sin. Antichrist.

Manna. special food or spiritual nourishment provided by God.

Mercy. in Hebrew, *hesed*; the compassion that causes one to help the weak.
Messiah. anointed one, in Greek *Christos*.
Micaiah. who is like God.
Michael. who is like God also.
Minister. a hireling who works for wages.
Mishael. Who is what God is?
Monotheism. one God.
Moses. drawn out, the national hero of the Hebrews, chosen by God Jehovah to deliver the Israelites from the Egyptian bondage, gave the Law through Moses.
Most High. El-Elyon.
Nazareth. hometown in lower Galilee of Mary and Joseph.
Nephilim. term applied to the giants during the pre-flood.
New Testament. more accurately rendered New Covenant, second part of the Holy Bible transcribing prophecy, and the lifetime and events from Jesus Christ onward.
Nimrod. hunter, ruler, founder of Nineveh.
Noah. means "rest," a righteous man and family God saved from the flood.
Noah's ark. rest in the ark, a vessel, the boat that carried Noah through the flood.
Obadiah. servant of Jehovah.
Obed. Worshiper or server.
Obeisance. to bow low or prostrate oneself.
Omnipotent. the ability of God to do whatever He wills.
Omnipresent. the ability by which God fills the whole universe in all its parts and is everywhere at once.
Omniscience. the attribute by which He knows perfectly all things which can be known, past present, and future.
Onan. strong.
Parable. a comparison of two subjects for the purpose of teaching a moral.
Paraclete. advocate.
Paradise. a park or forest or orchard.

Passover. one of the five festival feasts of the Hebrews, commemorates God's release from Egyptian slavery during the Exodus, instructed by God to put lamb's blood on the doorframe and lentil to protect the household.

Pastor. a shepherd, to feed, a clergyman in charge of a congregation.

Paul. the most pivotal and primary progenitor of our full gospel of the Grace and Truth of Jesus Christ, the new dispensation or covenant.

Pauline. my grandmother's name and the classification and term for Paul's gospel and writings.

Peace. a spirit of tranquility and freedom from either inward or outward disturbance, find rest in the Lord's peace.

Pentateuch. the Law or first five books of the old covenant, from creation to the end of the Mosaic era.

Pentecost. derived from the Greek meaning "fifty days when Holy Spirit fell on Pentecost," fifty days after the resurrection.

Perdition. perishing or the destruction.

Perfection. an absolute attribute of God alone; finished.

Persecution. strife in the life of and because of our *faith* in Christ Jesus.

Pestilence. any fatal epidemic often coming as a result of divine judgment.

Peter. means rock, originally named Cephas, chosen specially by Christ to lead and build on His church. Christ, however, is the official "rock" or chief cornerstone.

Pharisees. one of the three prominent Hebrew groups at the time of Christ—Sadducees, Pharisees, and the Essenes.

Philadelphia. brotherly love.

Philistines. Old Testament people of Palestine; Goliath, whom David slew, was a Philistine giant.

Philosophy. love of wisdom.

Piety. religious duty.

Praise. to exalt.

Prayer. to communicate with God. Prayer mixed with *faith* should be the daily business of every Christian. Martin Luther said, "A shoemaker makes a shoe, a tailor makes a coat, so also should a Christian pray."

Priest. one who is consecrated to and engaged in holy matters; one to do with the divine.
Principalities. the order of powerful angels and demons.
Promise. given to Abraham into a proto-evangelium and David, which he writes up in the Psalms.
Prophets. chosen of God to transmit His word, forthtelling and foretelling of future events as related to God.
Propitiation. to cover or atone for.
Proselyte. stranger.
Prostrate. to stretch out, with face on the ground in adoration and/or submission.
Providence. the universal sovereign reign of God.
Reconciliation. a change of relationship between God and man based on the redemptive work of Christ at the cross; He has changed it for us through Christ.
Ransom. a price paid for the redemption of a slave or captive, freeing him from captivity or possession.
Redeemed. to set right, to tear loose, or pay the ransom.
Religion. our recognition of our relationship to God and expressing that through *faith*, worship, and conduct.
Repentance. a resolute turning away and changing of your mind in reference to God, in light of His Grace to redeem us.
Reprobate. failing to do the test, moral corruption.
Resurrection. a raising, Christ's rising from the dead.
Revelation. the doctrine of God making Himself and relevant truths known to man.
Revile. to address with opprobrious or contumelious language, to reproach.
Reward. something given in recognition of an act.
Righteousness. the quality of rightness or justice.
Sabbath. cease, desist, rest.
Sackcloth. a dark coarse cloth, probably like burlap.
Sacrifice. a religious act belonging to worship, making an offering to God, to create or retain or celebrate friendly relations with the deity.
Sacrilege. to rob the temples, slandering God.

Sadducees. one of the three most common groups in Hebrew society at the time of Christ.

Salem. peace, name of a city at the time of Abraham where Melchizedek was the king and the high priest.

Salvation. deliverance from sin and condemnation, conversion, regeneration, justification, adoption, sanctification, and glorification!

Samaria. the ten northern tribes; they protested Rehoboam, rebuked for luxury and corruption, tribes of Israel.

Samson. one of the judges and heroes of ancient Israel.

Samuel. name of God or God hears.

Sanhedrin. the highest Jewish council during the Roman and Greek periods.

Saraph. noble one.

Satan. adversary, accuser, liar, father of the lie, devil, Beelzebub, deceiver, dragon, serpent, only allowed to go as far as God permits; fell from heaven through pride.

Saul. Israel's first king from 1050 BC to 1010 BC, reigned forty years.

Saul of Tarsus. Paul's name in the New Testament before his conversion on the road to Damascus.

Savior. deliverer, preserver, Jehovah alone is the savior through the title of the son Jesus Christ.

Science. knowledge.

Second Coming of Christ. the culmination and fulfillment of all prophecies to be completed at the end of this age, of which all signs are pointing toward.

Sakal. wise behavior or prudence; wisdom that leads to success.

Seed. agricultural, physiological, and figuratively.

Semites. derived from the peoples of Noah's son Shem.

Septuagint. the first of translations of the Old Testament from Hebrew to Greek.

Shekinah. the dwelling of God, the glory of His being.

Sin. anything in the creature to which does not express or is contrary to the holy character of the creator.

Spiritual gifts. extraordinary gifts of the spirit given to Christians to equip them for tasks specific.

Stripes. scourging and lashings of a beating or physical punishment.

Synagogue. Hebrew or Jewish place of assembly for worship.

Talmud. a collection of Jewish writings from the early centuries.

Temptation. any attempt to entice toward evil.

Temperance. self-control, chastity.

Testimony. solid solemn affirmation establishing some fact, a statement of one's Christian experience.

Testaments. more accurately translated as covenants.

Theocracy. a government in which God is the ruler, as with Israel and similarly with the believers in Jesus Christ, except for being under the New Covenant of the Grace and Truth of Jesus Christ and not the Mosaic Law.

Theology. the study of God and religious doctrines and matters of divinity.

Theophany. a visible appearance of God, usually in human form.

Timothy. honored of God.

Tobiah. Jehovah is good.

Tyndale, Wm. 1536 in English theologian, translated the Bible, executed.

Tongues. the gift of the Spirit, fell on all believers on the day of Pentecost.

Transfiguration. when Jesus was visibly glorified, witnessed by His three disciples, showing His inner glory while He was praying.

Transgression. rebellion or breaking of the law.

Tree of knowledge. tree beset in the middle of the garden as a test.

Tree of life. tree also in the garden; healing was in its leaves.

Tribulation. period of great suffering sent by God to punish rebellious men at the end of the latter days.

Trinity. three personalities of the Triune Godhead, Father, Son, and Holy Spirit; these three similitudes are one God, same in substance, equal in power and glory.

Truth. the correspondence of the known facts of existence with the sum total of God's universe: may be known by general and special revelation but only so much as God chooses to reveal.

God has made known all that is necessary for life and salvation. Truth is manifested supremely in Christ; those who turn away choose to live in error.

Undefiled. any person or thing not tainted with moral evil.
Uriah. Jehovah is light.
Uriel. God is light.
Uzzah. strong.
Uzzi. strong.
Uzziah. Jehovah is strength.
Uzziel. God is strength.
Unitarian. a denier of the trinity; only God and of Jesus.
Universalism. theological belief that all souls will eventually find salvation.
Utilitarianism. one who values things by their utility.
Via Delarosa. the sorrowful way, pathway to the cross.
Veracity. truth.
Vitalism. the doctrine that life in living organisms is caused by a force that is distinct from all physical and chemical forces.
Vision. sight presented to the mind through a dream; most convey a revelation of God.
Vow. a voluntary promise to God.
Watchmen. one who guards a city or a people or army.
Way. term for the path to God through Jesus Christ or the way of the Path Following Christ.
Wisdom. attribute of God; Jesus is wisdom.
Wrath. the anger of God against sinful people.
Word. one of the names of Jesus; He is the Word (John 1:1 and Genesis 1:1).
Worship. to bow down, to honor, of divine honors paid to a deity, to kiss or cherish in reverence.
Yahweh. God, Jehovah.
YHWH. the tetragrammaton, same as the above definition for Yahweh.
Yom Kippur. the day of atonement; the one day of the year when the high priest under the old Mosaic law would go in the temple and make atonement for the sins of the people.

Zachariah. Jehovah has remembered, two Zechariahs of note, one that came back from Babylon after the captivity with Zerubbabel and the Zechariah who was John the Baptist's father and a priest in the temple of and around the time of Jesus.
Zealot. one who is zealous, filled with zeal, highly spirited for the Lord.
Zebediah. Jehovah has remembered.
Zedekiah. Jehovah is righteous.
Zephaniah. hidden of Jehovah.
Zerahiah. Jehovah is/has risen.
Ziggurat. a temple tower, like Babel.
Zion. past, present, and future glory of Jerusalem; David brought the ark to Zion, the Mount of Olives, Mt. Mariah, Mount Carmel; used also for *heaven*.
Zuriel. whose rock is God.
Zurrishaddai. whose rock is the Almighty.

*****

One of the primary, if not even fundamental, concepts to be expounded on in this study will be to explore this subject or topic that Christianity was not a break from Judaism or the Hebrew religion, as many wrongly believe, but specifically, it was a planned evolution and continuation and the ultimate designed plan of Almighty God. For the former foreran the latter and ushered in, delivered, and established it.

Many through confusion and wrong understanding of God's overall plan believe that the Hebrew religion and Judaism and its offspring of Christianity are disconnected and of no relevance of one to the other. This could not be any further from the truth. From the list that I have compiled above of integral concepts, words, and phrases, there are three fundamental facts of God that need to be clearly understood and delineated here. Primarily, and first of all, God's omnipotence. His ability to do whatever He wills to do. Secondly, His omnipresence, which is the attribute by which He is able to fill the whole universe in all its parts and be everywhere at once.

And thirdly and most primarily, His omniscience. His attribute by which He knows perfectly all things which can be known, past, present, and future. God's omniscience through His divine intelligence, foreseeing, and foreknowing all eventualities and all possibilities which can be known revealed to God in His complete foreknowledge, every turn, choice, decision, and result of everything that the angels and humans, good and rebellious alike, would make in His realm of creation, which delivers to us very craftily both our free will and our plan for salvation, through our Lord and Savior Jesus Christ.

I must admit that the last paragraph dealt with, and expanded on, some pretty weighty information. It truly was not what I would describe as "milk and honey" information. However, it is a most necessary chunk of knowledge and quite revealing. Once you understand and establish these attributes of God, which were described above. It then becomes a baseline that opens certain *doorways* and paths to continued and further understanding. For in the very concept of what is God's omniscience, His very power of seeing the future clearly, through all possible eventualities, brings in an opening of understanding of just how His miraculous plan becomes possible, even probable, and you begin to see most clearly that little to nothing is left to mere chance or happenstance!

Given this information about our great Spirit being God, with these amazing powers and attributes, it is not a grand leap of *faith* as most perceive to grasp that such a being, with the ability to do anything that He desired, would choose out of His pure love and intelligence to create a family and give us free will and sacrifice tremendously to pay the ransom for our redemption. Using His power to redeem us and reconnect us in life and eternity back to Himself, ending our condemnation and removing any enmity or separation of us from Himself, God. Arriving at a finish that He clearly saw from the beginning, delivering His desired outcome, giving us a plan for our salvation and free will simultaneously delivering eternity with God in Heaven to us.

For with boldness, God says in Matthew 10:30, also in Luke 12:7, in Jesus's words, and He guarantees that He has an exact count of every hair we have on our heads constantly. This affirms and supports quite graphically, and emphatically, what a personal God that He is and how much He cares for, knows, and is willing to provide for and to us. Now set that down as your firm foundation and baseline from which we will build upon, taking a closer look at Jesus Christ's visitation to this earth, as we examine the qualities of Jesus Christ that God the Father desired to reveal to us through the incarnation and visitation.

Now we will take a look at some of the events that occurred in Jesus's life before He went to the cross at Calvary. I was aware previously, before my most intense research and study over the last two and a half to three years, that Jesus performed many miracles. I had not, before that, taken a very close examination of those or many other events in my early scripture exposure, and I went over things, and mistakenly so, much faster than I ever should have. That was folly on my part, and that is putting it mildly. For I want to say this with as strong of an emphasis as I possibly can. There are no small or insignificant details in the Bible. Every detail, description, number, and account of every story or parable in the whole book is significant and refers to something in the good Father's, our good shepherd's, most holy plan for mankind.

To bear out the statement above about how significant the details of the Bible are, I am going to introduce a few instances of just how that concept applies and at the same time provide you with this principle. So that you too will learn it and be able to apply it, and as you gain further understanding, and continue to expose yourself to God's Word. I referenced before in the early part of this book that as a boy, I was quite curious and was interested in science and was a somewhat bright youngster. I can say this unequivocally that every question I had about our existence—that is, the hows and the whys of us being here on this planet that I have pondered since a child—have all been answered, explained, displayed, played out, and recorded for us in the handiwork of God's love letter to us, His Holy Bible. Below will be a small list of numbers and what they symbolize or indicate in the parables, stories, and events of the Scriptures.

- 1 means or symbolizes unity with God
- 2 means or symbolizes in agreement with
- 3 means or symbolizes the resurrection

- 4 means or symbolizes the earth
- 5 means or symbolizes God's Grace
- 6 means or symbolizes man without God
- 7 means or symbolizes God's perfection or completion
- 8 means or symbolizes new or new beginnings
- 9 means or symbolizes Gods Holy Spirit
- 10 means or symbolizes completion
- 17 means or symbolizes victory
- 40 means or symbolizes testing or a period of testing
- 153 the number of fish they counted, there were likely more, when Jesus directed them, after fishing all night and getting nothing, to drop the net on the right side of the boat

A good display of applying the concept of numerical values of numbers being highly significant in the stories contained in the Scriptures will be to start right in on the number 153, as listed above. This is a good reference and application for the process that is used here and can be used in many of the parables, stories, and events recorded in the Bible. Above, the number 1 symbolizes unity with God. The number five symbolizes God's Grace with the number 3 meaning or symbolizing the resurrection. With this concept, you combine the meanings of the numbers together. If it's multiple digits, as it is in this instance combined here, the meaning is we have unity with God's Grace through the resurrection. That was the meaning of the 153 fish counted.

And it went way over my head for many years as to why they counted exactly 153 fish. Hopefully, that example helps to open your mind and broaden your perspective and allow you to see with a wider purview the critical detail that is very easy for a new believer or student of the word to not have any idea about and easily miss. As I have stated before, and I believe this helps to establish this fact and hone your recognition of it. There are no insignificant facts in the Bible. It is God's promised, and protected, divinely inspired message to all of us as He attempts to collect us (the willing) back to Himself for eternity through His Son Jesus Christ.

Now the direction will shift away for a portion of our study from focusing on Jesus's deity, His miraculous miracles performed and powers displayed, and move to more of a conceptual application of Christ's teachings, the message, and messages relayed to us by our Lord. Wisdom is the primary and key element of our character that we should desire and aspire to achieve. However, this is not wisdom in our own eyes, but G*odly, spiritual wisdom* is the specific goal we are to seek here. Proverbs 14:2–34 says:

> Whoever fears the Lord walks uprightly, but those who despise him are devious in their ways. A fools mouth lashes out with pride, but the lips of the wise protect them.

And now we will skip to verse 6:

> The mocker seeks wisdom and finds none, but knowledge comes easily to the discerning. Stay away from a fool, for you will not find knowledge on their lips. The wisdom of the prudent is to give thought to their ways, but the folly of fool is deception. Fools mock at making amends for sin, but goodwill is found among the upright. Each heart knows its own bitterness, and no one else can share its joy. The house of the wicked will be destroyed, but the tent of the upright will flourish. There is a way that appears to be right, but in the and it leads to death.

And we skip to this verse:

> The *faithless* will be fully repaid for their ways, and the good rewarded for the theirs. The simple believe anything, but the prudent give thought to their steps. The wise fear the Lord and shun evil, but a fool is hot-headed and yet feels secure. A quick tempered person does foolish things and the one who devises evil schemes

is hated. The simple inherit folly, but the prudent are crowned with knowledge. Evildoers will bow down in the presence of the good, and the wicked at the *gates* of the righteous.

And again, we will skip to verse 26:

Whoever fears the LORD has a secure fortress, and for their children it will be a refuge. The fear of the LORD is a fountain of life, turning a person from the snares of death.

And again, we skip to verse 31:

Whoever oppresses the poor shows contempt for their Maker, but whoever is kind to the needy honors God.

And now we skip to verse 34:

Righteousness exalts a nation, but sin condemns any people.

It was within the purpose of the last couple paragraphs that I was able to show, even if only just a small snippet of the wealth of knowledge and most specifically wisdom, that is available to us through the whole Bible. Unfortunately, many have discounted it as irrelevant and not being pertinent today or to have any real applicable value by stating such things as "the old has passed away" and now we only need the New Testament. While it (the New Testament) has delivered to us the complete and full gospel of our Lord and Savior Jesus Christ, by no means does that mean there is nothing of value or anything to be contributed to our knowledge, wisdom, and understanding of our plan of salvation from the "old."

On the contrary, I assert that without these richly demonstrated and contrived stories of God's people that reveal God's compassionate heart and plan to us, His redeemed people of *faith* in the risen Christ and to the people of Israel. The point that is being affirmed here is that you simply need to read the whole Bible, discounting none, as I have found in my walk toward His knowledge and wisdom, and I have observed this in many other devout believers most concretely.

The rabbinic traditions teach that Jehovah God decides on whether one is strong or weak, wise or foolish, and whether they are poor or rich, but not whether the individual will be righteous or wicked. That in short delivers the scenario that reveals that God leaves that to the desire of one's free will. This in my opinion reveals the very heart of the matter.

As you begin to be able to absorb and be saturated by the continued revealing of God's words of wisdom and His knowledge and the plans that He has for us, the ideal is that as these layers are being peeled away, digging further to get to the unequivocal truths, and as it did for me, the Bible literally has come alive, seamlessly substantiating itself and revealing a continuity of God in this reality and experience of ours in a way that I could never have completely imagined. Within those scriptures that were listed just above, on "righteousness exalting a nation," it reminded me of another Old Testament scripture that I have learned, "He who exalts himself, will be humbled, but he who humbles himself, will be exalted," as it says in Matthew 23:12, a very powerful scripture and one that I have been aware of for very many years.

And what it points to is one of the main concepts within the word of God and Christianity that is borne out by all of Christ's teachings and the example that has been given to us by Christ, denying oneself in the pursuit of godliness or us exampling His holiness. In other words, "Less of me, more of Christ." This, my friends, is an awareness, which is given by the Holy Spirit and will be revealed to you as it is to all believers as they become aware of the power and glory and the majesty of our mighty God and our Lord and Savior Jesus Christ. Profoundly here in 2 Corinthians 3:15–18, it says:

> Even to this day when Moses is read, a *veil* covers their hearts. But whenever anyone turns to

the Lord, their *veil* is taken away. Now the Lord is the Spirit, and where the Spirit of the Lord is, there is freedom. And we all, who with *unveiled* faces contemplate the Lord's glory, are being transformed into his ever-increasing glory, which comes from the Lord, who is the Spirit. (Holy Spirit)

There is another concept that we are going to explore here as we progress, firming up our understanding of Bible principles. There is a monumental revealing in truths of our human nature, as we have been created, that has become apparent and a major component in our understanding and application of God's plan of salvation for us. God is a spirit, and His scriptures instruct us to be able to communicate openly with the Father, we must also worship Him in spirit.

This concept is integral in the establishment of our worship of God. For some, this may not be a concept that has ever come across their awareness. It has mine. For what I have come to understand is that all the years that I was not aware of my spiritual nature and the need to recognize such to be able to commune and interact with our mighty God and that the other side of this coin that needs to be established is our human nature has two facets, the spiritual as I had previously mentioned and the flesh or our worldly nature. For this is no light matter.

Some may go about and live their whole lives, never having been made aware of this very fact and concept of our human nature. For until we recognize such a dichotomy in our own nature, which is exactly what the word of God has revealed to me, and I am certain many others too, we will not be able to discern our divine origin and our intended purpose. I'm now going to walk this out a good bit further. The flesh, our worldly nature, is the one that responds to our worldly desires, selfish interests, and our pursuits in our everyday existence apart from God.

This fleshly or worldly nature, as I have learned from God's Word, is in direct opposition and more explicitly in a constant battle or a warring against the spirit, or between rather, the two natures. As

THERE IS A DOORWAY...

I have learned over and over again, there is no substitute for God's Word. So for all clarity and purpose, let us go to His word on this subject. Galatians 5:13–24 says:

> You, my brothers and sisters, were called to be free. But do not use your freedom to indulge the flesh. Rather, serve one another humbly in love. For the entire Law is fulfilled in keeping this one command: "Love your neighbor as yourself. If you bite and devour each other, watch out or you will be destroyed by each other. So, I say, walk by the Spirit, and you will not gratify the desires of the flesh. For the flesh desires, what is contrary to the spirit, and the spirit, what is contrary to the flesh. They are in conflict, with each other, so that you are not to do whatever you want. But if you are led by the Spirit, you are not under the Law. The acts of the flesh are obvious: sexual immorality, impurity and debauchery; Idolatry and witchcraft; hatred, discord, jealousy, fits of rage, selfish ambition, dissensions, factions. and envy; drunkenness, orgies, and the like." "I warn you, as I did before, that those who live like this will not inherit the kingdom of God." "But the fruit of the Spirit is love, joy, peace, forbearance, kindness, goodness, faithfulness, gentleness and self-control. Against such things, there is no Law. Those who belong to Christ Jesus have crucified the flesh with its passions and desires. 25, Since we live by the Spirit, let us keep in step with the spirit. 26, let us not become conceited, provoking and envying each other."

And again, in Galatians 4:28–31, it says:

> Now you, brothers and sisters, like Isaac, are children of the promise. At that time the son born

> according to the flesh, persecuted the son born by the power of the Spirit, (Ishmael and Isaac). It is the same now. But what does Scriptures say? "Get rid of the slave woman and her son, for the slave woman's son will never share in the inheritance with the free woman's son." "Therefore, brothers and sisters, we are not children of the slave woman, but of the free woman."

In this instance, it is referring to the Old Testament story of Abraham's children Isaac and Ishmael and how God had promised Abraham a child of his own flesh. Abraham and Sarah in their advanced age began to lose *faith*, and instead of clinging to the words of God's promise, they gave in to what they perceived to be the realities surrounding them. And in their moment of unfaithfulness, Sarah orchestrated to have Abraham sleep with Hagar, the servant woman, for Sarah knew that she had been barren, and in their *faithlessness* to God, they chose not to wait on the promises of God.

Spiritually, what is typified here is this, Ishmael represents the flesh, while Isaac, the child born of God's promise, represents our spiritual nature. As stated before, the two natures are at war with each other, and as God says in His word, the son of the slave woman, represented by the flesh, and the son of the free woman, representing our spirit, and hence, the slave son, the flesh, can never share in the inheritance of God's promises given to those believers who worship in the spirit by Faith.

This event involving the two stepbrothers and the eventual split is the beginning of the Arab-Israeli strife and dissensions that continue to this day. Three scriptures will follow here to continue to bear this out. The first one is from 2 Corinthians 5:7, "For we live by *faith*, not by sight," then Galatians 3:24, "So the Law was our guardian until Christ came that we might be justified by Faith." And lastly here, Galatians 5:5, "For through the spirit we eagerly await by *faith*, the righteousness for which we hope." This *Faith* we speak of here is concretely the most vital, powerful, and critical element of the New Testament, second only to God Himself, for the whole Bible, and our salvation plan. It is not an action but a state of mind or even a "force of one's will."

The word *repentance* or "metanoyah" in Greek means a change or, in this instance, a change of mind or a turning away from a previous path to embark on a new one. This is exactly what we have here. We change course or direction or the path we were on to begin anew. When we leave our old ways, our sinfully controlled nature, and put on the new nature that we receive when we put on the garments of Christ by *Faith*, we accept His atonement for our sins, His gift of salvation to us, and the purging of all our sins, past, present, and future.

Yes, even the ones we have not yet committed. Not just for me, but the sins of the whole world. Trust me here, for our thrice-holy God, it was a vast overpayment. Yes, that is our great God. So revisiting on the primary and most pivotal element and a most powerful one that it is of our *Faith*, it is in Him, Christ Jesus, and here is why. In Hebrews 11:5–6, it says:

> By *faith* Enoch was taken from this life, so that he did not experience death; he could not be found, because God had taken him away. For before he was taken. He was commended as one who pleased God. And without *faith* it is impossible to please God, because anyone who comes to him must believe that he exists, and that he rewards those who earnestly/diligently seek him.

In Proverbs 1:7, and if I've mentioned it before, it's worth repeating, it says, "The fear of the LORD is the beginning of knowledge, but fools despise wisdom and instruction." Now that scripture there, I'm fairly certain, is self-explanatory and a critical plank in any platform of one's salvation. Proverbs 3:5–7 says:

> Trust in the Lord with all your heart, and lean not on your own understanding. In all your ways submit to him, and he will make your paths

straight. Do not be wise in your own eyes; fear the Lord and shun evil.

Romans 5:19 says:

> By one man's disobedience many were made sinners, so also by one man's obedience many will be made righteous.

For God is no longer demanding that we work for our salvation, only that we walk with Him in it! The Law was given by Moses. Grace and Truth came by Jesus Christ. It is the goodness of God that leads man to repentance. Christ is the end of the Law to all who believe. When we rest, God works, and when we work (or try to establish our righteousness by our performance), He rests! Our salvation is a gift from the divine! It is a simple beauty. He who knew no sin became sin so that we who were sin could become righteous. It is not the sinfulness of man that needs to be revealed. It is the righteousness of God that is needed to be revealed. God hates sin because He loves us.

The good news of the gospel is that we can receive the good that we don't deserve, that He first loved us, though we were yet sinners. Whatever is edifying imparts Grace, for the Law demands righteousness; under Grace, it imparts righteousness. It supplies. He is a better savior than we are sinners. *Faith* comes by hearing the word of God; fear comes by hearing the words of man. The Jewish sabbath was at the end of the week for sins. Christ was raised on the first day of the week to bless us through the week, not at the end! His Grace is attracted to our needs, and it flows in the worry-free areas of our lives. We need to live and to feed on fresh revelation; you are what *you* eat. As we know, Jesus is the bread of life. He is the living water.

What happened in the first garden was finished in another (Gethsemane). Our number one self-improvement plan is to live every day in a sense of His love for us—that is, walking in His Grace. He is the savior of our darkest hour. For it was during the fourth watch that He showed up in the midst of the storm. The resurrection is our divine receipt that all our sins were put away. He who was the richness of the universe became poverty so we who are poor through Him might become rich. Anything that is not of *Faith* is sin. Performance of the Law or works of any kind to establish one's own righteousness voids *Faith*, and inhibits the free flow of His *Grace* in our lives.

We only need to be washed once in the blood but over and over by the *water*. Just like in Exodus 12:12–13, in reference dually here, "When I see the blood, I will pass over you." This is specifically another one of the duality concept scriptures here, referring to both Passover night in Egypt and more ominously during the second coming of Jesus Christ as prophesied. John 6:40 says, "The will of God the Father is that everyone is to look to the Son believe in Him shall have eternal life and I will raise on the last day," which is wholly the result of the divine exchange of *Grace* and Peace.

We should let the peace of God rule our hearts and be thankful, and let His word dwell in us richly in all wisdom, teaching and admonishing with Psalms and hymns and singing, and with *Grace* and love in our hearts for the Lord in His name, giving thanks to the Father through Him. When we keep our eyes fixed on Jesus, the Holy Spirit goes to work. The Law came initially so we could see ourselves as sinners and understand our need for Christ. *Grace* makes you generous and opens your heart. He wants us to take all He has to give us. He loves us to take from Him out of His *Grace*. Remember, with God, it is more blessed to give than receive.

People generally do not want to talk about God because of their awareness of their sin and their sin debt. *Faith* when rooted removes this by the power of the Holy Spirit. For perfect love casts out fear. For when we love God in complete *Faith*, fear is removed, the debt paid, and we are no longer condemned. It is not our obedience that we are to be focused on but that our thoughts are to be focused on His obedience, which gets us to stop being dominated by our sin consciousness and shows us to look to Christ Jesus who is the author and finisher of our *Faith*, again keeping us focusing on His performance and righteousness and not either of those of ours because we have none.

For it is through Him that we have our redemption and salvation. His body was broken so that by the divine exchange, believers in Christ Jesus could be made well. In 1 Corinthians 3:6, it says, "He has made us competent as ministers of a New Covenant—not of the letter but of the Spirit; for the letter kills, but the Spirit gives life." In the gospels, Peter is well documented denying Jesus three times just as Jesus said he would. Did Jesus cast him off? No, quite the opposite in fact. When He appeared, He said, "Go and tell my disciples, and Peter!" even though He had said to Him, "Deny me before men, and I will deny you before my Father!" Also in 2 Peter 1:5–9, it says:

> For this very reason, make every effort to add to your *faith* goodness; And to goodness knowledge; and to knowledge, self-control; And to self-control, perseverance; And to perseverance, godliness; and to godliness, mutual affection; And to mutual affection, love. For if you possess these qualities in increasing measure, they will keep you from being ineffective and unproductive in your knowledge of our Lord Jesus Christ. but whoever does not have them is near sighted and blind, forgetting that they have been cleansed from their past sins.

A constant and recurring theme throughout the New Testament is the need for us to become aware of the love of the Father, not our love for Him but rather His love for us, also that we are accepted and completely forgiven because Jesus has already been judged in our place. God's holiness and justice are why He, as God, cannot condemn us. For again as I stated before, the Passover lamb's blood that protected the Israelites once prior on *doorposts* has now been applied directly to us today who *believe*. We are blessed because God's forgiveness will never impute sin to us.

He cannot. Its price has already been paid. Staying on the gospels and visiting again with Peter, we reflect on the scene in the boat on the water, where he saw Jesus walking on the water in the distance, and he asks Jesus, "Bid me come?" As Peter began to go to Jesus, he kept his eyes on the Lord, and he was progressing walking as Christ did on top of the water. But the moment Peter became *distracted* by the wind and the waves and the surrounding storminess, once his eyes came off Jesus, he began to sink. This was an actual happening, as well as a metaphor for us. This is another example of the concept of duality.

When we come to our Father, *believing*, lowly, and humble, just as the woman with the issue of blood did as she pressed against Jesus in the crowd, He forgives our doubt and answers our *Faith*. For you cannot get under the shadow of the Almighty unless you draw close to Jesus. Whatever drives us to God is good, for it gets us to look at Him and shows us our needs. And through my inadequacies, I have learned to depend on God. This allows God to use us to the maximum of our potential. He will help you do whatever He calls you to do.

If I may be so bold, I can attest to this very concept here, right now, of myself. With the power of the Holy Spirit, He has filled me and assisted me along the way of me and Him writing this book, from beginning to end, to glorify Almighty God (El Shaddai). For I can do all things through Christ Jesus my Lord who strengthens me. In 2 Corinthians 8:9, it says:

> For you know the Grace of our Lord Jesus Christ, that though He was rich, yet for your sake He became poor, so that you through His poverty might become rich.

And in Hebrews 5:8–14, it says:

> Son though he was, he learned obedience from what he suffered and, once made perfect, he became the source of eternal salvation for all who obey him and was designated by God to be high priest in the order of Melchizedek. we have much to say about this, but it is hard to make it clear to you because you no longer try to understand. In fact, though by this time you ought to

be teachers, you need someone to teach you the elementary truths of God's word all over again. You need milk, not solid food! Anyone who lives on milk, being still an infant, is not acquainted with the teachings about righteousness. But solid food is for the mature, who by constant use have trained themselves to distinguish good from evil.

Joy and insecurity in the Lord cannot coexist. God wants us to come to Him without any fear, fully assured of our *faith*, which is the antidote for sin, and for us to know that He is on our side. We do not look to our wounds or transgressions, rather we are to look to Jesus Christ our Savior and the atoning sacrifice He has performed in our place, instead of, and for us. When it comes to the Gospel of Jesus Christ, there is no compromise; it is the power and the Gospel of Grace and Peace. Our Lord Jesus was forsaken at the cross so that we could be received by the Father, once our sins had been covered, accounted as paid for, and thus, repositioning us as right in our standing with the Father.

As we have identified through God's Word, man's nature is fallen and sinful. Therefore, we need the righteousness of God to cover us. This happens through the immense redemptive sacrifice God performed before all mankind. By God's *Grace*, we have justification by *Faith* in the Son whom the Father sent. He who knew no sin, who did no sin, who in Him was no sin became sin, so we, who have done no right thing, might become *righteous*. Jesus Christ was the most restful person ever. When we rest in Him, He works. And when we work, He rests! God gives pain to the doubter and pleasure to the believer for *faith* is confidence in God and comes to us when we hear God talk. In all these things, be strong and of courage, praying, meditating, and *believe* supplicating the Father on all things. For meditation is *reading* His Word.

Believe and understand what you have read.
Absorbing the knowledge and wisdom.
Apply it to our lives.
Absorb and follow God's Word.

THERE IS A DOORWAY...

Faith is when fear is smothered by your belief in God's Peace, Love, and His Righteousness. For perfect *love* casts out all fear. Our Lord promises to never leave us *believers* or will He ever forsake us. Once saved, we are saved indeed. It is from *faith* to *faith* to *faith*. Anything that is not of *Faith* is *sin*. We *believers* are the righteousness of God in Christ Jesus. He came bringing us Sonship because of God's desire for a family. Only *Grace* can give us this inheritance, making us heirs of the world and this universe with Jesus as our *redeemer*.

One of the most pivotal and moving teachings that I have learned about the life of Jesus that was very consequential in my breakthrough of fuller understanding was the most loaded and powerful information that was contained in the messages of the first two miracles that Jesus performed. As I have stated previously and have been informed of by many Bible scholars that there are no insignificant details in the Bible—God's word to us. Given that, it is inherently integral to our understanding of the depth of detail availed to us in scripture.

During the first miracle Jesus performs at the wedding festival, the wine runs out, and He turns the tall jars of water into wine, and not just any wine, but the best or finest wine. From the time one begins to plant a vineyard, it takes approximately ten to eleven years to get to what would be considered fine wine. So with the waving of a hand, Jesus was able to, within a second of time, condense eleven years into a single moment to yield the finest of wines. With the first miracle, He was showing us that He is the God of time.

The second miracle Jesus performed was the healing of the royal official's son. This He performed from two cities away. When the royal official traveled back home for a whole day, he arrived to find his servants running to tell him the boy was well, and when the royal official asked when he turned for the better, they answered that it was yesterday near sunset—exactly when Jesus told the royal official his son was well and would live.

My friends, this was our God displaying before all the world's eyes that he is the Creator that wove the time and space continuum together. Once I digested these truths and discerned the preponderance of them, my life would never again be the same. As a mechanically minded, science-based individual, God had now hit me dead center of my radar screen, armed with the truth of God.

These scriptures and words of knowledge of our Lord are just a sprinkling of some of the gems and pearls of wisdom that are laced throughout this book and similarly the Bible. My intention is not to do all the study and research for you. It is to direct you and to get you to pick up God's Word and to help you to understand further the power, truth, glory, and the majesty it contains, even the complete knowledge and explanation of our existence. So search, read, saturate, and bathe yourself daily in His pure and holy wisdom—the Bible, His Word. That is where He reveals Himself to us.

Chapter 3

The Good Shepherd

This chapter will delve into one of the most powerful and demonstrative picture messages of the Bible. We will examine, study, and attempt to discern and apply this imagery and its pictorial message and application, specifically how it exposes the tenderness and depth of God's love for us. For me, it was one of the second or third scriptures that I learned and attested to memory, and that is the 23rd Psalm. And I quote from that:

> The LORD is my shepherd, I lack nothing. He makes me lie down in green pastures, he leads me beside quiet waters, He restores my soul. He leads me along the path of righteousness for His name's sake. even though I walk through the valley of the shadow of death, I will fear no evil, for you are with me; your rod and your staff they comfort me all along the way. You prepare a table before me in the presence of my enemies. You anoint my head with oil; my cup overflows. Surely your goodness and love and *Grace* will follow me all the days of my life, and I will dwell in the house of the Lord forever.

That was likely the first time in my life, and in my growth in His word, that I had come across or began to be aware of the reference to the good *shepherd*. At that time, I did not have a lot to tether the concept to, only the awareness and the reference to a special tender of the sheep. Now, I did know of the symbology of Jesus as the lamb of God, however, even though the shepherd was sometimes in the photo or figurines. The greater symbology of *the good shepherd* and how it applies to us had somehow gotten by. No longer.

It has been over these many years of learning that the concept of the good shepherd has continually revealed itself through this and many other scriptural references to being one of the most illuminating and rich revelations of our loving God and His intimate care and protection of us, His well-protected sheep. Truly in this instance, the KJV does this verse much more justice in its interpretation, and it speaks to me in my walk toward God. That is why I mixed the KJV and NIV above for it delivers the messages with more clarity. "He restores my soul. He leads me in paths of Righteousness for His names sake" (3). Now right here is where the rubber meets the road for this expounds on the mysterious concept of *righteousness*. And it needs clarity in its meaning, how we understand, and how we employ it.

We are instructed to seek His (God's or Christ's) righteousness, not our own, as so often the misinterpretation of this is taught. As far as our righteousness goes, we have none on our own merit. For we have a fallen nature since the actions of Adam in the garden of Eden nor were we ever able to keep all ten of the commandments given perfectly. Hence, God's divine plan of salvation, first typified by animal blood for the removal of sins, was then ultimately established, concluded, and founded in the Law of Grace and Truth of Jesus Christ, which has released His *Grace* unto all who will *believe* in Him in the world, which was included in His divine plan—initially established with His chosen people, Israel, and in God's foreknowledge, knowing they (Israel) would reject Him (Christ) and the new dispensation He attempted to instruct them on and put them under and to remove the Mosaic Law.

He then chose Paul to take this message to the rest of the world, the Gentiles, upon Israel's rejection. All of which was in God's foreknowledge and divine plan. This is the part of what is exhibited in God's plan that helps to deliver our option of free will by His design. We will eventually be merged back into one people at the conclusion of things—one people, all the children of God, with God after Jesus Christ's second coming, which is what the word *Emmanuelle* means, "God who is with us." In Revelation 21:3–4, He says:

> And I heard a loud voice from the throne saying. "Look! God's dwelling place is now among the people, and He will dwell with them. They will be His people, and God Himself will be with them and be their God. He will wipe every tear from their eyes. There will be no more death or mourning or crying or pain, for the old order of things has passed away."

This is not pie in the sky. This is for us, all who choose to *believe* the words of God and in the Son whom He sent. It certainly cannot be lost on practically anyone with any basic knowledge of the Bible, or at least it should not be, that King David was initially a shepherd boy—the same shepherd boy who slew the giant Goliath of the Philistines. This was not merely a coincidence. What has been provided in the New Testament as well as the old is a delivery system of picture messages that have been orchestrated, directed, and produced by Almighty God for the storied display and direction of mankind and God's plan for it. It will be the effort of this examination of this chapter to peel away at these layers of depth and richness that so boldly declare God's purpose, desires, and provisions that He has made for us.

Our part in this orchestration as *believers* is not a complicated one. For as the Gospel of Jesus Christ clearly describes, we as *believers* are justified and sanctified by our *belief* in our Lord and Savior Jesus Christ, the Messiah, and His finished work on the cross. For even though we were yet sinners, as it says in John 3:16, which was the first scripture I learned at age eleven when I was saved as stated in an earlier chapter, "For God so loved this world that he gave his only begotten son, that whosoever should *believe* in Him shall not perish, and have everlasting/eternal life." This act of benevolence and self-sacrifice is the very epitome of a protecting, guiding, and loving shepherd over His flock—the ultimate *good shepherd*.

There is certainly no coincidence in my mind that this very scripture is the one that began my path of learning, sanctified me, and began the long process of illumination and enlightenment into God and the knowledge of our Lord and Savior Jesus Christ. He protects His sheep, even laying His life down to save them.

The outset of any large undertaking, certainly, one as large as attempting to read, understand, and learn about the mysteries of our existence through the Bible is probably as large and as daunting of an undertaking that one could immerse themselves in. It certainly is not a mystery to me at this point in my life at fifty-nine years of age that the quest was as elusive, challenging, yet ever so worthy. As to whether I placed any effort or emphasis on my part to arrive at this revelatory level of understanding, I do not. It was consistently through the reading and study of the Old Testament and New that I began to understand the intense and graphic nature of the stories of the Bible were intentional as they helped map out and indelibly impress the pictorial message of the lives of God's people, which most of the time were actual events yet symbolic of coming events of the Messiah.

For with the foreknowledge of God, being the Alpha and the Omega or the Aleph and the Taph, the beginning and the end as it is, our good Father has intrinsically woven His wisdom, combined with knowing all things and all possible eventualities into the very fabric and complete delivery of our reality as we know it; all these provisions and creations are the handiwork of Jehovah God to deliver the world and the so-called proving ground where the desires of God's heart and ultimate purpose of achieving a family who loves and worships Him and all His glory of their own accord.

Yes, we must remember God who foreknew all things, what the angels would do, the giants, evil people and good alike, the Hebrews, the Gentiles, all, and in the foreknowing of all this, He yet devised the plan of this reality as we know it, where God took part of Himself to create His only son, the firstborn of all creation, to reveal His love, character, and thrice Holy Spirit to us all, and in so doing, inviting and consecrating us as children into His eternal family.

For it says in Colossians 1:15–20:

> The Son is the image of the invisible God. The first-born of all creation. For in him all things were created: things in heaven and on earth, visible and invisible, whether thrones or powers or rulers or authorities; all things have been created through Him and for Him. He is before all things, and in Him all things hold together. And He is the head of the body, the church; He is the beginning and the first-born from among the dead, so that in everything He might have *supremacy*. For God was pleased to have all of His fullness dwell in him, and through him to reconcile to himself all things, whether things on earth or things in heaven, by making peace through his blood, shed on the cross.

So easily projected then, He is gravity. He is Light. Jesus Christ is the ultimate reality. The complete expanse of the total creation, from one edge of the expanding universe to the other, as He is that great shepherd and we *believers* are His sheep. This is top-level information of the first kind, and it is not easily revealed or unloaded in a short time. But as for myself, the Holy Spirit has laid a foundation and continued to layer me with knowledge revealed through His word to me directly or in any way accessible. God is a *spirit*. We must grow and worship in spirit, as we are exposed to these important truths. Now, as we have established, the world calls to our fleshly desires. The Holy Spirit draws our spirit toward His.

As Joseph Prince says, "For it is the goodness of God that leads man to repentance, not the goodness of man that brings salvation from God." And this scripture is found in Romans 2:4, where it says: "Or do you show contempt for the riches of his kindness, forbearance, and patience, not realizing that God's goodness/kindness is intended to lead you to repentance." And John 3:13 further states:

> No one has ever gone to heaven except him, the one who came from heaven,—the Son of Man. Just as Moses lifted-up the snake in the wilderness, the Son of Man must be lifted up, so that everyone who believes may have eternal life in him.

Matthew begins the New Testament. In chapter 2, where it is describing the Jewish Messiah's birth, recounting the Old Testament prophecy, it says in Matthew 2:6, "But you, Bethlehem, in the land of Judah, are by no means least among the rulers of Judah: for out of you will come a ruler who will shepherd my people Israel." Just before that in chapter 1, an angel of the Lord appeared to Joseph. Mary, Jesus's mother, was betrothed to Joseph to wed when the Angel Gabriel appeared to Mary telling her she had found favor with God and that she would conceive a son and name Him Yeshua. He will be a God with us, "Immanuel," and save His people from their sins.

The angel of the Lord appeared to Joseph in a dream and said in Matthew 1:20–21:

> Do not be afraid to take Mary as your wife, because what is conceived in her is from the Holy Spirit. She will give birth to a son, and you are to give him the name Yeshua in Hebrew, which means Salvation, and translates to Jesus in English, because he will save his people from their sins.

The story of the shepherds watching over the flock tending the sheep is interwoven all throughout the prophecy of the coming Messiah. The nativity in Bethlehem and the announcing of the angels to the shepherds watching of over the flocks in the field is told in Luke 2:8–21:

And there were shepherds living out in the fields nearby, keeping watch over the flocks at night. An angel of the Lord appeared to them, and the glory of the Lord shone around them, and they were terrified. But the angel said to them, do not be afraid. I bring you good news that will cause great joy for all the people. Today in the town of David a Savior has been born to you; you will find a baby wrapped in clothes and lying in a manger. Suddenly a great company of the heavenly host (Angels) appeared with the angel, praising God and saying, "Glory to God in the highest heaven and on earth peace to those on whom his favor rests." (*Grace*) When the Angels had left them and gone into heaven, the shepherds said to one another, "Let's go to Bethlehem and see this thing that has happened, which the Lord has told us about." So they hurried off and found Mary and Joseph and the baby, who was lying in the manger. When they had seen him. They spread the word concerning what had been told them about this child, And all who heard it were amazed at what the shepherds said to them. But Mary treasured up all these things and pondered them in her heart. The shepherds returned, glorifying and praising God for all the things they had heard and seen, which were just as they had been told. On the eighth day, when it was time to circumcise the child, he was named Jesus, (Yeshua, Joshua, or Yashua actually in Hebrew) the name the angel had given him before he was conceived.

This is just a small sprinkling of the shepherd's references as I have begun to unveil them for they are used continually in both the Old and the New Testaments. This picture is constantly and consistently delivering to us the comforting and beautifully reassuring message from our Father God as our good shepherd.

This may be a very revealing fact on my part, but as a boy, and I'm not certain where it originated, I am going to assume from my father and somehow down from the lineage to him, but as a boy when I would fall asleep at night or have difficulty attempting to, the method I recall and was taught or had suggested to me was strangely enough, to count sheep. Now, having a very vivid and active imagination, I was quite adept at setting up the scenario in my mind as I attempted to drift off to sleep.

In this mental vision, I would picture the corner of a fenced pasture, with hundreds of sheep corralled toward the corner of the pen, and in this scenario, I would systematically watch and count one by one as the little woolly critters jumped over and out of the pen one by one. Strange, no. Odd, no. Coincidence, likely not. Purposeful and aiding in the overall pictorial God has illustrated for us, yes, certainly, for it is one of the most effective displays of God's care and love for us in showering His *Grace* on us in the story of the good shepherd and his sheep.

The *good shepherd and his sheep* in John 10:1–30 begins and reveals this concept of the teaching virtually, as well as any.

THERE IS A DOORWAY...

Very truly I tell you Pharisees, anyone who has not entered the sheep pen by the *gate*, but climbs in by some other way, is a thief and a robber. The one who enters by the *gate* is the Shepherd of the sheep. The gatekeeper opens the *gate* for him, and the sheep listen to his voice. He calls his own sheep by name and leads them out. When he has brought out all his own, he goes on ahead of them, and his sheep follow him because they know his voice. That they will never follow a stranger; in fact, they will run away from him because they do not recognize a stranger's voice. Jesus used this figure of speech, but the Pharisees did not understand what he was telling them. Therefore, Jesus said again," very truly I tell you, I am the *gate* for the sheep. All who have come before me are thieves and robbers, but the sheep had not listened to them. I am the *gate*; whoever enters through me will be saved. They will come in and go out and find pasture. The thief comes only to steal and kill and destroy; I have come that they may have life and have it to the full. 11." I am the good shepherd. The good shepherd lays down his life for the sheep. The hired hand is not the Shepherd and does not own the sheep. So, when he sees the wolf coming, he abandons the sheep and runs away. Then the wolf attacks the flock and scatters it. The man runs away because he is a hired hand and cares nothing for the sheep. "I am the good shepherd; I know my sheep and my sheep know me—Just as the Father knows me and I know the Father—and I lay down my life for the sheep. I have other sheep that are not of this sheep pen. I must bring them also. They too will listen to my voice, and there shall be one flock and one shepherd. The reason, my father loves me is that I lay down my life—only to take it up again. No one takes it from me, but I lay it down of my own accord. I have authority to lay it down and authority to take it up again. This command I received from my Father.

And further after some other discussions, Jesus adds in verse 25 after they questioned His purposes:

"If you are the Messiah tell us plainly." Jesus answered, "I did tell you, but you do not *believe*. The works, I do in my Father's name testify about me, But you do not *believe* because you are not my sheep. My sheep listen to my voice; I know them, and they follow me. I give them eternal life, and they shall never perish; no one will snatch them out of my hand. My Father, who has given them to me, is greater than all; no one can snatch them out of my Father's hands. I and the Father are one."

In Luke's gospel is another very powerful parable or moral message delivery story that was recounted to me by Pastor Joseph Prince out of this gospel expounding on the story of the lost sheep. And it begins in Luke 15:3–7:

Then Jesus told them this parable; "Suppose one of you has a hundred sheep and loses one of them. Does he leave the 99 in the open country and go after the lost sheep until he finds it? And when he finds it, he joyfully puts it on his shoulders. And goes home. Then he calls his friends and neighbors together and says, rejoice with me; I have found my lost sheep. I tell you that in the same way there will be more rejoicing in heaven over one sinner who repents than over 99 righteous persons who do not need to repent.

Now, it would seem rather complete as a compact and effective parable at this point, but as Pastor Prince elaborated on, there is more to flesh out here. Jesus has revealed to us in person and word that He is sent from the Father and at one with Him as His only begotten Son and the promised comforter, His Holy Spirit and as prophesied in the Old Testament text and confirmed in all Scripture. He is the good shepherd, and we are the lost sheep. He leaves the flock for us, the lost ones. He searches us out. He finds us where we are. He rescues us. He picks us up and carries us on His shoulders. He cares for and comforts us. He takes us home. He calls His friends and neighbors rejoicing over the once lost but now found member of His personal flock of which He obviously cares a great deal for.

Now here is *Grace*. In all this, what was the requirement of us (the sheep) in this story? There was none. Other than to allow ourselves to be carried, to rest on the good shepherd's shoulders, to *believe* in His care, love, and comfort, and to rest peacefully in His protection, resting in our Heavenly Father. Yes, my friends, this is exactly how good, loving, committed, and caring our Lord is, and He provides us in His word the proofs to help evidence to us His handiwork and love for us, His creation. In James 5:11, it says:

> As you know, we count as blessed those that have persevered. You have heard of Job's perseverance and have seen what the Lord finally brought about. The Lord is full of compassion and mercy.

We will be continuing to elaborate on the theme of the good shepherd, which we shall do to some great length, as I have previously mentioned, for it is one of the most graphic, demonstrative, and effective pictorial messages, displaying the Father's love for His *believing* people. In Jesus's second appearance to the disciples after the resurrection at the Sea of Galilee, while they were fishing, it sets up our next encounter with the application of the analogy and description of the good shepherd. It is at this encounter by the Sea of Galilee along the seashore that Jesus uses the shepherd analogy and picture message to implore Peter and, I assume, as well as the others in attendance of the importance of their pastoral duties to the new church and just how important and what emphasis Jesus placed on this.

The heading above this subsection of chapter 21 of the book of John is "Jesus reinstates Peter." Jesus has just appeared on shore as this group of disciples had been fishing most of the night and caught nothing. They did not realize that it was Him, and He called to them. In chapter 21 of John, verses 5–6, it says, "'Friends haven't you any fish?' 'No,' they answered. He said, 'Throw your net on the right side of the boat and you will find some.'"

When they did, they were unable to haul the net in because of the large number of fish. It was just after this that the exchange between our Lord Jesus and Peter occurred. It picks up again in verses 15–19, still in chapter 21:

> When they had finished eating, Jesus said to Simon Peter, "Simon son of John, do you love me more than these?" "Yes, Lord, he said, you know that I love you." Jesus said, "Feed my lambs." Again, Jesus said, "Simon son of John, do you love me?" He answered, "Yes Lord, you know that I love you." Jesus said, "Take care of my sheep." The third time, He said to him, "Simon son of John, do you love me?" Peter was hurt because Jesus asked him the third time, do you love me? He said, "Lord, you know all things; you know that I love you," Jesus said, "Feed my sheep. Very truly I tell you, when you were younger, you dressed yourself and went where you wanted; but when you are old, you will stretch out your hands, and someone else will dress you and lead you where you do not want to go." Jesus said this to

indicate the kind of death by which Peter would glorify God. Then he said to him, "Follow me."

Jesus completely embodies the qualities and the role of the good shepherd over His sheep, or rather His flock. For it is without any equivocation of the fact of just how important and how central to the mission entrusted to Peter that God takes His role as our good shepherd.

As Jesus walks with the disciples daily for over three years, He imputes to them through miraculous healings, parables, and discussions His message of the kingdom of God and the purpose of His first coming. The analogy of our Lord Jesus as the good shepherd throughout the whole Bible is the most used and accurate portrayal of our loving creator Almighty God. In Matthew 9:35–38, it says:

> Jesus went through all the towns and villages, teaching in their synagogues, proclaiming the good news of the kingdom and healing every disease and sickness. When he saw the crowds, he had compassion on them, because they were harassed and helpless, like sheep without a shepherd. Then he said to his disciples, "The harvest is plentiful, but the workers are few. Ask the Lord of the harvest, therefore, to send out workers into his harvest field."

The method and effort of conveyance here are in the repetition, the preponderance of the evidence in the scriptures, and the propensity of knowledge and wisdom that *faith* exudes that has been revealed by the *Grace* of the Holy Spirit that plants, waters, and cultivates the word by God's miraculous powers, directed to those that *believe* that He is.

The good shepherd analogy is so much more than, and more powerful than, any average story or parable. For contained within the pictorial message are a plethora of layers of meaning and ever-revealing moralist and factual basis of the length, breadth, width, and depth of the love of God and the kingdom of heaven that He has provided for us to inherit as His believing children. In Matthew 25:31, we get a glimpse into God's heart, where in this scripture, it is quite simplified in a way where it simply appears as just another analogy or subtle parable about a teaching or concept of the word.

No, rather subtly, in small, soft words and phrases, it delivers to us our complete reality, the reason for existence, and the culmination of world history and future as God has designed, instituted, and conducted, being the creator and originator of all things. Matthew 25:31–46 says:

> When the Son of Man comes in his glory, and all the angels with him, he will sit on his glorious throne. All the nations will be gathered before him, and he will separate the people one from another as a shepherd separates the sheep from the goats. He will put the sheep on his right and the goats on his left. Then the King will say to those on his right, "And you who are blessed by my Father; take your inheritance, the kingdom prepared for you since the creation of the world. For I was hungry, and you gave me something to eat, I was thirsty, and you gave me something to drink, I was a stranger and you invited me in. I needed clothes and you clothed me, I was sick, and you looked after me. I was in prison and you came to visit me. Then the righteous will answer him, Lord, when did we see you hungry and feed you, or thirsty and give you something to drink? When did we see you a stranger and invite you in, or needing clothes and clothe you? When did we see you sick or in prison and go visit you? The King will reply, truly I tell you, whatever you did for one of the least of these brothers and sisters of mine, you did for me. Then he will say to those on his left, "Depart from me, you who are cursed into the eternal fire prepared for the devil

and his angels. For I was hungry, and you gave me nothing to eat, I was thirsty, and you gave me nothing to drink, I was a stranger, and you did not invite me in, I needed clothes and you did not clothe me, I was sick and in prison, and you did not look after me. They will also answer, Lord, when did we see you hungry or thirsty or a stranger or needing clothes or sick or in prison, and did not help you? "He will reply, truly I tell you, whatever you did not do for one of the least of these, you did not do for me." "Then they will go away to eternal punishment, but the righteous to eternal life."

Make no mistake, the righteousness spoken of here are us believers in Jesus Christ, the Messiah, who have been made righteous by our belief in Jesus, as prophesied in Old Testament scriptures from the very start in Genesis 1:26:

> Then God said, "Let us make mankind in our image, in our likeness, so that they may rule over the fish in the sea and the birds in the sky, over the livestock and all the wild animals, and over all the creatures that move along the ground."

The *us* referred to in verse 26 is God the Father and His only begotten son Jesus Christ, and His Holy Spirit, and I will back that up from John 1:1–14, which is captioned in my NIV Bible, "The Word Became Flesh."

> In the beginning was the Word, and the Word was with God, and the *Word* was God. He was with God in the beginning. Through him all things were made; without him nothing was made that has been made. In him was life, and

that life was the light of all mankind. The light shines in the darkness, and the darkness has not overcome it. There was a man sent from God, whose name was John. He came as a witness to testify concerning that light, so that through him all might believe. He himself was not that light; he came only as a witness to the light. The true light that gives light to everyone was coming into the world. He was in the world, and though the world was made through him, the world did not recognize him. He came to that which was his own, but his own did not *receive* him. Yet to all who did *received* him, to those who *believed* in his name, he gave the right to become children of God—Children born not of natural descent, nor of human decision or a husband's will, but born of God. The word became flesh and made his dwelling among us. We have seen his glory, the glory of the one and only son, who came from the Father, full of *Grace* and Truth.

It was intentional above, in the last paragraph and scripture reference, that I did not elaborate, define, or clarify what was included in the previously mentioned scripture simply because it is in straightforward, simplistic language and needs no interpretation. For some scriptures are more direct and straightforward than others that take a bit more discernment. Many prophecies of the Old Testament are foretold and predicted, or rather prophesied, about the coming of our Lord and Savior Jesus Christ. A great deal of the scripture contained in the Psalms, which were written by King David and are what we call messianic, indicating the coming Messiah.

This simply means they are prophetical in nature and prophesy of the coming of the Messiah as the root of the word implies. For many years, this was a most confusing area of study for me as I had not been imbued with the wisdom and knowledge at that time to have the full flow of God's story and all the applicable pieces to the grand mystery, or the Lord's puzzle, that I was in the process of putting together.

As elusive as it was, and for many different reasons, I am so thankful to Almighty God that He did not give up on continuing to put knowledge and His teaching in my path. For many years, He filled me to a saturation point as it were to where the knowledge of His word and His wisdom were finally able to overtake the damage that had been done by wrong doctrine and instruction that was prevalent in the churches I attended in my earlier years, as well as the distractions of my flesh put before me by myself or the one called the tempter.

I truly was the one lost sheep that the good shepherd left His other ninety-nine for, and He kept hunting and calling and waiting for me till He got through, and for that, I am so blessed and eternally grateful to the one Jesus revealed to us as Father or "Abba." In Matthew 2:6, it refers to an Old Testament prophesy, "But you, Bethlehem, in the land of Judah, are by no means least among the rulers of Judah; for out of you will come a ruler who will Shepherd my people Israel." In Mark, He references the keeper of us sheep, again with deep care and compassion for them. Mark 6:30–34 says:

> The apostles gathered around Jesus and reported to him all they had done and taught. Then, because so many people were coming and going that they did not even have a chance to eat, he said to them, "Come with me by yourselves to a quiet place and get some rest." So they went away by themselves in the boat to a solitary place. But many who saw them leaving recognized them and ran on foot from all the towns and got there ahead of them. When Jesus landed and saw a large crowd, he had compassion on them, because they were like sheep without a shepherd. So he began teaching them many things.

Another scripture from Psalms fits very well here in reference to the messianic prophesies of the Psalms. In Psalms 77 and 78, there are several references in these messianic scriptures that forward the good shepherd aspect here. Psalms 77:19–20 says:

> Your paths lead through the city, your way through the mighty waters, though your footprints were not seen. You led your people like a flock by the hand of Moses and Aaron.

It is the *exodus* out of Egypt that these verses are referencing. Again, in Psalms 78:50–53, it says:

> He prepared a path for his anger; he did not spare them from death but gave them over to the plague. He struck down all the firstborn of Egypt, the first fruits of manhood in the tents of Ham. But he brought his people out like a flock; he led them like sheep through the wilderness. He guided them safely, so they were unafraid; but the sea engulfed their enemies.

Jehovah God was revealing to King David that through his lineage, the Messiah, the *savior* of the world, is going to come and be the deliverer of His people in a similar fashion of the freeing of God's people from their captivity in Egypt. Another shepherd reference is found in the same book of Psalms in the same area or group of chapters. In Psalms 78, it says:

> He chose David his servant and took him from the sheep pens; From tending the sheep he brought him to be a shepherd of his people Jacob, of Israel, his inheritance. And David shepherded them with integrity of heart; with skillful hand's he led them.

THERE IS A DOORWAY…

What is being asserted here by God to us in these Psalms and stories about King David is the beautiful pictorial message, and an ever-indelible message at that, that God so effectively uses when trying to convey this message to us. Just as David, who was a shepherd boy and becomes the king of Israel, was handpicked and tailored by God's own fashioning to become and symbolize the good shepherd, our Lord and Savior Jesus Christ and Father God over all of us His sheep, we should allow Him to be our good shepherd and our God. For we cannot access and approach the Father unless we first believe that He exists.

At this point is my intention to steer the direction and emphasis of this next group of scriptures and stay in the Old Testament. In Genesis 49, starting in verse 22, the verses speak of Joseph who is another character God uses to typify and emulate characteristics of His coming Messiah Savior and Son to the world. In another one of His pictorial messages about the portraying of the coming Christ in the book of Genesis. Here are a few of the traits that typify the duality and application of this scripture and with references through Joseph directly toward Jesus Christ.

They are both beloved sons as revealed in the scriptures. They were both the most special children. Both were hated and rejected by their brothers and their peers. With Jesus, He was sacrificed on the cross, crucified, buried, and raised on the third day. Joseph was thrown in the pit. They did not kill him, and similarly, he eventually got out. For Jesus, He came to His own people, and they did not recognize Him. With Joseph, when his brothers had journeyed down to Egypt and were presented before him, they did not recognize him as their brother.

Jesus was betrayed by Judas for thirty pieces of silver. With Joseph, he was sold by his brothers to the Medianite merchants for twenty shekels of silver. It is in this very same method of analogy that is used through many, if not all, chronicling of the events of the Hebrew people throughout the Old Testament, that God is using to reveal His very heart and nature, that He holds for us through the recording of these events.

Now on with Genesis 49:22–26, it says:

> Joseph is a fruitful vine, a fruitful vine near a spring, whose branches climb over a wall. With bitterness archers attacked him; they shot at him with hostility. But his bow remained steady, his strong arms stayed limber, because of the hand of the mighty one of Jacob, because of the Shepherd, the rock of Israel, because of your fathers God, who helps you, because of the Almighty, who blesses you with blessings of the skies above, blessings of the deep springs below, blessings of the breast and womb. Your father's blessings are greater than the blessings of the ancient mountains, then the bounty of the age-old hills. Let all these rest on the head of Joseph, on the brow of the prince among his brothers.

There is a lot to dig into in reference to Joseph and the importance of his story and how powerful the display of the imagery is. There are powerful and interesting similarities in the story of Joseph and how just exactly it compares and is related and pointing forward directly to Jesus Christ, the coming Messiah. And certainly not to be lost in the references to this group of scriptures is how they typify in very many ways the coming Messiah and the sprinkling of references to the good shepherd at the same time. As it appears here, I may be able to take down two birds with one stone.

In verse 24 of Genesis 49, it refers to the mighty one of Jacob, whom we know God changed his name to Israel after Jacob had wrestled with the man all night (likely the appearance of a theophany) and after besting this assumedly unknown man just before daybreak. As the man requested for Jacob to let him go, Jacob requests that the man bless him. Now it has taken many years of study and learning and getting in tune with the flow of God's Word, the Bible, and just what and how many different fashions that He tries to get His point or story containing messages across to us.

Seeing just how long it has taken for me to understand this story line in the Old Testament, from the first time that I had read it until now, I think somehow it easily went over my head about the fact that after wrestling with the man in the scripture that I'm referencing, apart from Genesis 49 that was slightly earlier in Genesis, in chapter 32 verse 22, it talks about this wrestling match that Jacob (Joseph's father) had with an unnamed man. What I gleaned was that this event in Genesis 32:22 was that the man that Jacob wrestled with was a manifestation of Jehovah God as a man (theophany) more accurately and specifically.

It was Jesus Christ in His preincarnate being. There He became a man that night and wrestled with Jacob, touching his hip and injuring it, which would make him limp for the rest of his life. After making an agreement with Jacob to let him go, He gave him back the blessing that was taken through deception by Esau. The appearance of God as a human in the Bible is what is called a *theophany*. This is another building block in the stepping-stones that the Old Testament established, developing out the story of Israel as God's chosen people as they are the vehicle that chronicles, moves, and delivers the Messiah, the Savior of the world, Jesus Christ, His Holy Spirit, God.

Now moving on from Genesis and on into one of the major prophets Ezekiel. I have come upon a very rich resource in chapter 34, which is titled or captioned, "The Lord will be Israel's Shepherd." At this point, I will not pick this scripture apart, for I feel it is a part of the journey of this book that there is some understanding or accumulation of knowledge of the Bible that is being built up in your foundation of understanding, and for that reason, I am going to excerpt the whole chapter of 34 and transcribe it directly. For it speaks mightily well on its own, as God's Word always does. I will join in the commentary after its presentation. Ezekiel 34:1–31 says:

> The word of the LORD came to me: Son of Man, prophesy against the shepherds of Israel; prophecy and say to them: This is what the Sovereign LORD says: Woe to you shepherds of Israel who only take care of yourselves! Should not shepherds take care of the flock? You eat the

curds, clothe yourselves with the wall of slaughter of the choice animals, but you do not take care of the flock. You have not strengthened the weak or healed the sick or bound up the injured. You have not brought back the strays or searched for the lost. You have ruled them harshly and brutally. So they were scattered because there was no Shepherd, and when they were scattered, they became food for all the wild animals. My sheep wandered over all the mountains and on every high hill. They were scattered over the whole earth that no one searched or looked for them. "Therefore, you shepherds, hear the word of the LORD: As surely as I live, declares the Sovereign LORD, because my flock lacks a Shepherd, and so has been plundered and has become food for all the wild animals, and because my shepherds did not search for my flock, but cared for themselves rather than for my flock, therefore, you shepherds, hear the word of the LORD: This is what the sovereign Lord says: I am against the shepherds and will hold them accountable for my flock. I will remove them from attending the flocks so that, the shepherds can no longer feed themselves. I will rescue my flock from their mouths, and it will no longer be food for them."

"For this is what the Sovereign LORD says: I myself will search for my sheep and look after them. As a Shepherd looked after his scattered flock when he is with them, so will I look after my sheep. I will rescue them from all the places where they were scattered on the day of clouds and darkness. I will bring them out from the nations and gather them from the countries, I will bring them into their own land. I will pasture them on the mountains of Israel, in the ravines and in all the settlements in the land. I will tend them in good pasture, and the mountain heights of Israel will be their grazing land. There they will lie down in good grazing land, and there they will feed in a rich pasture on the mountains of Israel. I myself will tend my sheep and have them lie down, declares the Sovereign Lord. I will search for the lost and bring back the strays. I will bind up the injured and strengthen the weak, but the sleek and the strong I will destroy. I will Shepherd the flock with justice. As for you, my flock, this is what the Sovereign Lord says: I will judge between one sheep and another, and between rams and goats. Is it not enough for you to feed on the good pasture? Must you also trample the rest of your pasture with your feet? Is it not enough for you to drink clear water? Must you also muddied the rest with your feet? Therefore, this is what the Sovereign Lord says to them: see, I myself will judge between the fat sheep and the lean sheep. Because you shove with flank and shoulder, butting all the week sheep with your horns until you have driven them away, I will save my flock, and they will no longer be plundered. I will judge between one sheep and another. I will place over them one Shepherd, my servant David, and he will tend them; he will tend them and be their Shepherd. I the Lord will be their God, and my servant David will be prince among them. I The Lord has spoken."

"I will make a covenant of peace with them and rid the land of savage beasts so that they may live in the wilderness and sleep in the forest in safety. I will make them and the places surrounding my hill a blessing. I will send down showers in season; there will be showers of blessings that will

> prove to be. The trees will yield their fruit, and the ground will yield its crops; the people will be secure in their land. They will know that I am the Lord, when I break the bars of their yoke and rescue them from the hands of those who enslaved them. They will no longer be plundered by the nations, nor will wild animals devour them. They will live in safety, and no one will make them afraid. I will provide for them the land renowned for its crops, and they will no longer be victims of famine in the land or bear the scorn of the nations. Then they will know that I, am the Lord their God, and with them in that day, the Israelites, are my people, declares the sovereign Lord. You are my sheep, the sheep of my pasture, and I am your God, declares the Sovereign Lord."

Wow. That is an amazing chapter in Ezekiel. This whole chapter 34 is a very powerful display of the messianic prophecies. It also displays the beautiful pictorial message of God as our good shepherd, ever tending to us, His flock, and the prophetic display of the plans that He has for His sheep in the land that He gave them.

The next scripture that I will reference here is found in Ecclesiastes 12:9–13:

> Not only was the teacher wise, but he also imparted knowledge to the people. He pondered, and searched out, and set in order many proverbs. The teacher searched to find just the right words, and what he wrote was upright and true. The words of the wise are like goads, they are collected sayings like firmly embedded nails—given by one Shepherd. Be warned my son, of anything in addition to them. Of making many books there is no end, and much study wearies the body. Now, all has been heard; here is the conclusion

of the matter: Fear God and keep his commandments, for this is the duty of all mankind."

So a goad is a tool used to dig mud out of an oxen cart or plow of sorts, and "firmly embedded nails" speaks of things being firmly held together. Inferred herein then is a confirmation of the importance of gaining godly wisdom and that the words of the wise have been assembled for us by one shepherd to use as the tools to navigate our struggles and the wisdom to help hold our existence together. Amen.

Wow, initially, in my prep work for this chapter in these verses of Scripture we are referencing here, I had planned to stop at verse 12, which would have been a mistake. It was at the bottom of the page and where it just naturally stopped. Upon further study, I realized that the final verse 13 in this group of scriptures that was over on top of the next page was profound and most conclusive on this and many matters. The phrase here I quote, "Fear God and keep his commandments, for this is the duty of all mankind" is a most powerful and loaded directive. This scripture is taken from the Old Testament of the Bible and is written or given to the Hebrew people, the people of Israel.

It has a timeless and present application in the lives of all *believers*, even today, for we have new commands now, as we *believe* in the Son whom the Father has sent. In days of old, before the Messiah had come, there was a different set of prime directives, or *the commandments*, given by God Jehovah, through His servant Moses. For as it says in John 1:17–18:

> For the Law was given through Moses; *Grace* and Truth came through Jesus Christ. No one has ever seen God, but the one and only son, who is himself God, and is in the closest relationship with the father, has made him known.

Now we are no longer under the Law, but we are under the *Grace* and Truth of Jesus Christ, as displayed by Christ's life and death and the finished work at the cross. All prophecies fulfilled. Backing this assertion up is the scripture found in Romans 13:8–10, which is titled "Love Fulfills the Law":

> Let no debt remain outstanding, except a continuing debt to love one another, for whoever loves others has fulfilled the Law. The Commandments, you shall not commit adultery, you shall not murder, you shall not steal, you shall not covet, and whatever other command there may be, are summed up in this one command: "Love your neighbor as yourself. Love does no harm to a neighbor. Therefore love, is the fulfillment of the Law.

Our spirits come to us from the breath of God. All the requirements for us by God were fulfilled in Jesus Christ. We *believers* will reap what Jesus has sown for us and released at the cross. Salvation is nothing more than our consenting to God to be saved through our Lord and Savior Jesus Christ. Well-fed sheep become *good shepherds*.

Chapter 4

We Are Saved by Grace through Faith

We are transformed by beholding the glory of our God. For 2 Peter 1:2–9, it says:

> *Grace* and peace be yours in abundance through the knowledge of God and of Jesus our Lord. His divine power has given us everything we need for a Godly life through our knowledge of Him who called us by His own glory and goodness. Through these He has given us His very great and precious promises, so that through them you may participate in the divine nature, having escaped the corruption in the world caused by evil desires. For this very reason, make every effort to add to your *faith* goodness; and to goodness, knowledge; And to knowledge, self-control; and to self-control, perseverance; and to perseverance, godliness; And to godliness, mutual affection: and to mutual affection, love. For if you possess these qualities in increasing measure, they will keep you from being ineffective and unproductive in your knowledge of our Lord Jesus Christ. But whoever does not have

them is nearsighted and blind, forgetting that they have been cleansed from their past sentence.

We as a people, our human race, had been condemned in the garden of Eden by the act of disobedience of Adam. Where God said, "That man will, by the sweat of his brow gather his food." From then onward, sin entered the world and death also, which had not been there originally in the garden of paradise prior to Adam's disobedience of eating from the fruit of the tree of the knowledge of good and evil, which symbolizes the Mosaic Law, as it declares in the opening book of Genesis in the Holy Bible. It is this event that begins the requirement of a need for our *salvation*. From the fallen nature we inherited, from their (Adam's and Eve's) acts in the garden, which has caused our fall from our prior standing before God.

The word *gospel* means truth or the good news and comes from the root word *God-spell*. One of the most powerful concepts of the gospel is the fact that it tells of the good news that we can receive. A good that we do not deserve. For since through one man's disobedience, Adam's sin entered the world and through the *divine exchange* of God's Son, Jesus Christ and His death on the cross, He who was completely without sin received our punishment and our condemnation in our place, revealing that Jesus was God's *Grace* personified. Jesus is the tree of Life.

Through this act, the one perfect being who knew no sin, did no sin, and in Him, there was no sin became sin so that we, who have done no right thing, may become *righteous* by our *believing* in Him and the finished work at the cross. This was necessary due to God's completely good and thrice-holy nature. For as it says in scripture without the shedding of blood, there can be no remission of sin, and that was established by Jehovah God in the Mosaic Law, and previously in the Garden of Eden, all of which was a forerunner and a foreshadowing of what was to come ultimately in the appearance in our world of our Savior Jesus Christ. For what was under that Mosaic covenant was through the sacrificial requirements of temple worship and ceremonial temple rites were actual and yet symbolic foretelling in a pictorial message of the ultimate atonement of Jesus Christ as revealed through the Old Covenant economy.

It is under this economy of the Old Testament scriptures that God is revealing His divine plan His heart and very nature of our Almighty God and just how much He loves us His children. For it says in Hebrews 11:6, "And without *faith*, it is impossible to please God, because anyone who comes to him must *believe* that he exists and that he rewards those who earnestly seek him." In Titus 3:7, Paul, in his writings, also affirms this, "So that, having been justified by his *Grace*, we might become heirs having the hope of eternal life." Again, here in Romans 3:19–26, it affirms and gives evidence of this quite clearly. This is a hard-to-understand concept of how the Mosaic Law was done away with at the cross of Jesus Christ.

> Now we know that whatever the Law says, it says to those who are under the Law, so that every mouth may be silenced and the whole world may be held accountable to God. Therefore, no one will be declared righteous in God's sight by the works of the Law; rather, through the Law we become conscious of our sin. But now apart from the Law. The righteousness of God has been made known, to which the Law and the prophets testify. This righteousness is given through *Faith* in Jesus Christ to all who *believe*. There is no difference between Jew and Gentile, For all have sinned and fall far short of the glory of God, And all are justified freely by his *Grace* through the redemption that came by Christ Jesus. God presented Christ as a sacrifice of atonement, through the shedding of his blood—to be received by *Faith*. He did this to demonstrate his righteousness, because in his forbearance he had left the sins committed before-hand unpunished—He did it to demonstrate his righteousness at the

present time, so-as-to be just, and the one who *justifies*, those who have *Faith* in Jesus.

In my estimation, one of the main contributors to stumbling and a hindrance to my understanding was the misuse and misapplication of the Mosaic Law and the Ten Commandments, how it is taught, and its meaning and ultimate limited purpose. For the Law itself was never able to save anyone. The mechanism primarily was used to expose and make us aware of sin. All the ceremonial rites and procedures associated with the sacrifices and ordinances of the Law were an archetype of the final and ultimate sacrifice necessary for the redemption of our souls—that is, our salvation, which was performed by the choice Jesus Christ made of laying His life down to redeem us for the remission of our sins.

This was accomplished by the shedding of Jesus Christ the Messiah's blood in accordance with the Mosaic Law and the ultimate fulfillment of that prophecy. The book of Isaiah was written approximately eight hundred years before the birth of Christ in Bethlehem. Isaiah and David, although David was a king, were both prophets in the Old Testament, with Jesus Christ being a descendent of the bloodline of King David, which had also been prophesied that the Messiah would be a descendent and the lion of the tribe of Judah. Isaiah's prophecy is most profound, with much messianic knowledge and prophetical information included within.

Also, the Psalms are filled with many other messianic prophecies and insights into the house of which David was the king. The lion of the tribe of Judah. King David wrote the Psalms, and Solomon wrote Proverbs. Again, much of the Psalms that David wrote were messianic in nature, revealing much of the truth and information of our Lord and Savior Jesus Christ who was yet to appear. Many of David's Psalms are quoted in the New Testament, helping to establish the prophetical and messianic nature of the Psalms, which reveal some of the mystery that is to come in Him, fulfilling the Law and the prophets with His walking on this earth, the miracles He performed, and the knowledge imputed to us by Him and His followers, our fellow *believers*, our brothers and sisters in Christ Jesus.

THERE IS A DOORWAY...

In Acts 2:29–36, Peter is addressing the Hebrew people and says:

> Fellow Israelites, I can tell you confidently that the patriarch David died and was buried, and his tomb is here to this day. But he was a prophet and knew that God had promised him on oath that he would place one of his descendants on his throne. Seeing what was to come, He spoke of the resurrection of the Messiah, that he was not abandoned to the realm of the dead, nor did his body see decay. God has raised this Jesus to life, and we are all witnesses of it. Exalted to the right hand of God, He has received from the father the promised Holy Spirit and has poured out what you now see and hear. For David did, not ascend to heaven, and yet he said, "the Lord said to my Lord; "sit at my right hand, Until I make your enemies a foot stool for your feet." Therefore let all Israel, be assured of this: God has made this Jesus, whom you crucified, both Lord and Messiah.

One of the most profound occurrences at the time of Christ's visitation was the supplanting and deliverance from the Law and the Ten Commandments. Once Jesus Christ laid down His life for us, crucified on the cross, He also nailed the Law and the Ten Commandments to the cross at the time of His death for the divine exchange, installing the Law of God's *Grace*, which by our *faith*, we are saved through that said *Grace*, and He affirms this by the final decree before He expired when He said in John 19:30, "When now, he had received the sour wine. Jesus said: 'It has been accomplished (Finished) and bowing his head. He delivered up his spirit."

Now, it is at this time and point in this work that I would like to suggest, after affirming through much study, that it was completed with the occurrence of His resurrection on the third day, conquering over sin and death what 1,500 years of killing bulls and calves could never achieve—redemption, justification. It is through this colossal act that Jesus Christ accomplished, and our *belief* in those very facts delivers to us, our salvation, completed by His work for us on the cross. And that we add absolutely nothing to that.

This reconciles us back to the Father as it says in Ephesians 2:8–10:

> For it is by God's *Grace* you have been saved, through *faith*-and this is not from yourselves, it is the *gift* of God. Not by works, so that no one can boast. For we are God's handiwork, created in Christ Jesus to do good works, which God prepared in advance for us to do.

Here again, as the scriptures say in Paul's message to the Romans in 4:20–25 of Abraham:

> Yet he did not waver through *unbelief* regarding the promise of God but was strengthened in his *faith* and gave glory to God, being fully persuaded that God had power to do what he had promised. This is why, "It was credited to him as righteousness." the words "it was credited to him" were written not for him alone, but also for us, to whom God will credit righteousness—for us who *believe* in him who raised Jesus our Lord from the dead. He was delivered over to death for our sins and was raised to life for our *justification*.

This preeminent concept is further reinforced in Romans 5:1–2:

> Therefore, since we have been justified through *faith*, we have peace with God through our Lord Jesus Christ, through whom we have

gained access by *faith* into this *Grace* in which we now stand. And we boast in the hope of the glory of God.

For it is not the sinfulness of man that needs to be revealed but the righteousness of God. Our salvation transcends this reality, and it is a gift to us from the divine, which is why it has been hidden from the wise and the prudent, for it resides in our *faith* in Jesus Christ, which avails our righteous standing before God, not wise, righteous. For no one can fake *faith* before God. For He is the great Holy Spirit who knows all things. We are called to live in *faith* and to gain godly wisdom and to seek His kingdom and His righteousness, and all these things will be added unto us. Thus, it is most straightforward and clear.

Once we repent and accept through *faith* Christ and the cross, we are made righteous. We become Jesus Christ's righteousness by our *Faith* in Him. "For by *Grace* you are saved through *Faith*, so that none may boast." In 1 John 2:12, the author John says, "I am writing to you, dear children, because your sins have been forgiven on account of his name." "For Christ is the end of the Law to all who *believe*. For this God is righteous by making us righteous." Clearly then, this most amazing God of ours has devised, engineered, and created this very clever existence of ours in a most specific and purposeful way.

He is revealing to us His majesty, plan, and undeniable wisdom and intelligence through His living word, the Holy Bible, within which there is no discrepancy, error, or untruth of any kind but only the holiest and most perfect plan for our existence and salvation and future, as only our great God could devise and produce for us in our Bible. It was created in a way that bears out His story, or *history*, as transcribed from God to the writers, prophets, apostles, and witnesses, as He directed them to write in the past of the future mysteriously as only God could, foreknowing all possibilities and eventualities.

It has been the intended direction of this chapter to lay some groundwork from the New Testament of the most beautiful element that is displayed to us by God, His love for us displayed through His *Grace*. However, this concept of God's *Grace* does not appear for the first time in the New Testament. There are very many instances of God's *Grace* in the Old Testament. In the next group of scriptures that we will examine, we will take from the Old Testament to help bear out this concept of God's *Grace* and how it establishes there that it had been revealed 420 years before Moses gave the Law on Mt. Sinai, even further back to Abel as stated in Genesis and is referenced here in Hebrews 11:1–40, with the entire chapter to follow here:

> Now *faith* is confidence in what we hope for and assurance about what we do not see. This is what the ancients were commended for. By *faith* we understand that the universe was formed that God's command, so that what is seen was not made of what was visible. By *faith* Abel brought God a better offering than Cain. By *faith*, he was commended as righteous, when God spoke well of his offerings. And by *faith* Abel still speaks, even though he is dead. By *faith* Enoch was taken from this life, so that he did not experience death: "He could not be found, because God had taken him away." For before he was taken, he was commended as one who pleased God. And without *faith* it is impossible to please God, because anyone who comes to him must *believe* that he exists and that he rewards those who earnestly seek him. By *faith* in Noah, when warned about things not yet seen, in holy fear built an Ark to save his family. By his *faith* he condemned the world, and he became heir of the righteousness that is in keeping with *faith*. By *faith* Abraham, when called to go to a place he would later receive as his inheritance, obeyed and went, even though he did not know where he was going. By *faith*, he made his home in the promised land like a

stranger in a foreign country; he lived in tents, as did Isaac and Jacob, who were heirs with him of the same promise. For he was looking forward to the city, with foundations, whose architect and builder is God. And by *faith* even Sarah, who was past childbearing age, was enabled to bear children, because she considered Him *faithful* who had made the promise. And so from this one-man, and he as good as dead, came descendants as numerous as the stars in the sky, and as countless as the sand on the seashore.

All these people were still living by *faith* when they died. They did not receive the things promised; they only saw them and welcomed them from a distance, admitting that they were foreigners and strangers on earth. People who say such things show that they are looking for a country of their own. If they had been thinking of the country they had left, they would have had opportunity to return. Instead, they were longing for a better country—a heavenly one. Therefore God is not ashamed to be called their God, for he has prepared a city for them. By *faith* Abraham, when God tested him, offered Isaac as a sacrifice. He who had embraced the promises was about to sacrifice his one and only son. Even though God had said to him. It is through Isaac that your offspring will be reckoned. Abraham reasoned that God could even raise the dead, and so in a manner of speaking. He did receive Isaac back from death. By *faith* Isaac blessed Jacob and Esau, in-regard-to-their future. By *faith* Jacob, when he was dying, blessed each of Joseph's sons, and worshiped as he leaned on top of his staff. By *faith* Joseph, when his end was near, spoke about the exodus of the Israelites from Egypt and gave instructions concerning the burial of his bones. By *faith* Moses' parents hid him for three months after he was born, because they saw he was no ordinary child, and they were not afraid of the Kings edict. By *faith* Moses, when he had grown up, refused to be known as the son of Pharaoh's daughter. He chose to be mistreated along with the people of God rather than to enjoy the fleeting pleasures of sin. He regarded disgrace for the sake of Christ as of greater value than the treasures of Egypt, because he was looking ahead to his reward. By *faith* he left Egypt, not fearing the Kings anger; he persevered because he saw him who is invisible. By *faith* he kept The Passover and the application of blood, so that the destroyer of the firstborn would not touch the firstborn of Israel. By *faith* that people passed through the Red Sea as on dry land; but when the Egyptians tried to do so, they were drowned. By *faith* the walls of Jericho fell, after the army had marched around them for seven days. By *faith* the prostitute Rahab, because she welcomed the spies, was not killed with those who were disobedient. And what more shall I say? I do not have time to talk about Gideon, Barak, Samson and Jephthath, about David and Samuel and the prophets, who through *faith* conquered kingdoms, administered justice, and gained what was promised; who shut the mouths of lions, quenched the fury of the flames, and escaped the edge of the sword; whose weakness was turned to strength; and who became powerful in battle and routed foreign armies. Women received back their dead, raised to life again. There were others who were tortured, refusing to be released so that they might gain an even better resurrection.

> Some faced jeers and flogging, and even chains and imprisonment. They were put to death by stoning; they were sawed in-two; they were killed by the sword. They went about in sheepskins and goatskin's, destitute, persecuted and mistreated—The world was not worthy of them. They wandered in deserts and mountains, living in caves and in holes in the ground. These were all commended for their *Faith*, yet none of them received what had been promised, since God had planned something better for us that only together with us, would they be made perfect.

I have here used the same method that Paul employs in taking the whole of chapter 11 in Hebrews completely out and inserting it here. By doing so, I am piggybacking from his approach to show the contemporaries at the present time, as Paul was teaching, that this primary, fundamental element and concept of us *believers* in this Gospel of being saved by His (Jehovah God's) *Grace* through our *Faith* in Jesus Christ our God—Father, Son, and Holy Spirit—was in place and evidenced from the very beginning and established in the Old Testament, that this chapter with its preponderance of *believers* in God, one after the other, take Him at His word and *believe* through *faith* in the words He spoke to them of the promises of God and just how powerful that actual history is.

For it is the goodness of God that leads us to repentance. It says in Matthew 22:14, "For many are invited, but few are chosen." This quote is used to wrap up the parable told by Jesus of *the wedding banquet*. As with a lot of scriptures in the Old Testament, the New Testament also similarly is a collection of picture messages of the history of God's people Israel first and also the telling of and displaying the story of our God the Father and His Son Jesus Christ and His crucifixion, resurrection, and ascension on high to the right hand of the Father and is seated in heaven, having completed the finished work of the Cross, releasing His Holy Spirit to supply the *believing* world with the *Grace* that He so longs to share with us *believers*, His adopted children by *Faith* in the Messiah, our Lord and Savior, sent from the Father for the redemption of all *believers*—those that receive of Holy Spirit, the revelation of Jesus Christ, God's Word, and then *believe*.

After revealing the balance of the gospel message to Paul, which began after the Holy Spirit appeared to him on the road to Damascus and in the mountains of Arabia and then further Revelation to John on the island of Patmos, where He also appeared before the apostle whom Jesus loved, John, to whom He revealed the overarching plan to the end of the age, the whole book of Revelation, it says in Colossians 1:9–14:

> We continually ask God to fill you with the knowledge of his will through all the wisdom and understanding that the Spirit gives, so that you may live a life worthy of the Lord and please him in every way: bearing fruit in every good work, growing in the knowledge of God, being strengthened with all power. According to his glorious might so that you may have great endurance and patience, in giving joyful thanks to the Father, who has qualified you to share in the inheritance of his holy people in the kingdom of light. For he has rescued us from the dominion of darkness and brought us into the kingdom of the son he loves, in whom we have *redemption*, the forgiveness of your sins.

It was completely the purpose of the Law to make us aware and inform us of the consequences of sin, God's stand on it, and the ramifications of disobedience. Conversely, through the Law of *Grace*, it is the righteousness of God that is revealed to us by our reconciliation to Him through *Faith* in God's Son, who laid down His life for us, redeeming us and taking on the punishment we so rightly would deserve. A price for all sin had to be paid for God's righteousness and justice to be upheld and permanently established, and through God's plan, His Holy Son, the Christ, became the propitiatory sacrifice for all who will receive this most incredible gift from the Father of all to us. Our salvation resides in our *Faith* in God the Father and His Son Christ Jesus, whom He sent in exchange for all our sins.

It avails to us our righteous standing before God. For we now live under Jesus Christ's established Law of *Grace*, washed clean in His shed blood as a remission for the sins of the *believer*. The new dispensation was put into place once the finished work of the Cross was completed. Romans 10:17 says, "Consequently, *faith* comes from hearing the message, and the message is heard through the word about Christ." Just a bit earlier in the same chapter, Paul explains the failure of the Mosaic Law's effectiveness, and just where it was, that under the Law, they presumed their own righteousness when there was none. Romans 10:1–4 says:

> Brothers and sisters, my heart's desire in prayer to God for the Israelites, is that they may be saved. For I can testify about them that they are zealous for God, but their zeal is not based on knowledge. Since they did not know the righteousness of God and sought to establish their own, they did not submit to God's righteousness. Christ is the culmination of the Law so that there may be righteousness, for everyone who *believes*.

Amen!

So then what is God's will? Let us look it up in the word. Matthew 7:21–23 says:

> Not everyone who says to me, Lord, Lord, Will enter the kingdom of heaven, but the one who does the will of my Father who is in heaven. Many will say to me on that day, Lord, Lord, did we not prophesy in your name and in your name drive out demons and, in your name, perform many miracles? Then I will tell them plainly, "I never knew you, away from me you evildoers."

Now in my natural blunt, head-on, normal, and pragmatic approach. Asked and answered. Here then, profoundly simple, straightforward, and most exacting. It says in John 6:40–51:

> For my father's will is that everyone who looks to the Son and *believes* in him shall have eternal life, and I will raise him up at the last day.

And again, picking up in the verse:

> "Stop grumbling amongst yourselves," Jesus answered. "No one can come to me unless the Father who sent me draws them, and I will raise them up at the last day. It is written in the Prophets: They will all be taught by God. Everyone who has heard the Father and learned from him comes to me. No one has seen the Father except for the one who is from God; only He has seen the Father. Very truly I tell you, the one who *believes* has eternal life. I am the bread of life. Your ancestors ate the manna in the wilderness. Yet they died. But here is the bread that comes down from heaven, which anyone may eat and not die. I am the living bread that came down from heaven. Whoever eats this bread will live forever. This bread is my flesh, which I will give for the life of the world."

And John 1:17 says, "For the Law was given through Moses; *Grace* and Truth came through Jesus Christ." That is as straightforward, powerful, and direct as anything I have ever read, obviously much clearer now and evermore so as my study, sermon listening, from edifying and knowledge revealing sources, has increased. On this, you must be very careful. To fight for and protect this *Faith* we have, which is only consistently revealed in the love of God for us and the redeeming blood of Christ and our *Faith* of that alone, *Grace* is freely given. We must only *believe* and *receive*. Not even confession because then it is no longer free. Remember the lost sheep only consented to the shepherd to allow him to carry it.

The name of God (Jehovah) as His identity was known in the Old Testament—not by all but sometimes only by a select few of the rabbis, Pharisees, and Sadducees. For there were periods of time when the sacred name of God was kept secret, unknown to the general population of the Hebrews, and held as sacred knowledge only for the select or elect few, even to a point where the Jewish leaders believed that the sacred name of God should not ever even be uttered.

In the Hebrew alphabet, there are no vowels and only twenty-two consonants. The holy name of God appeared as four letters—YHWH—what is known as the tetragrammaton. It is with this identity that God had revealed Himself in the days past before Christ's first coming, besides being the Great I Am or the "I Am That I Am" as He revealed to Moses on Mt. Sinai at the burning bush. In Hebrew, that was said roughly as Yahweh and was translated to English and was derived into the word we know as *Jehovah* in our language by the adding of vowels that we have in our English alphabet and was the accurate name in the Old Testament of God.

A very profound scripture that it is, again, found in Romans 10:17 has been pivotal in this evolution of my spiritual growth and understanding, and yes, I am repeating it. For I *believe* this has been guided directly by the Holy Spirit. I perceive, for there is no other way that I could have received it. "Consequently, *Faith* comes from hearing the message, and the message is heard through the word about Christ."

This repeat is intentional. Initially, this scripture and group of words lacked true definition in my understanding, which is now much more on point with the true gospel, as not revealed by Jesus Christ to all twelve apostles but only to Paul, as his was the freshest, newest, and last word given before the last book of Revelation was given to John on the island of Patmos while he was in exile. There is the Law of *Faith* that God established most clearly through Paul's writings. And in Hebrews, he speaks volumes of how this same *Faith* was established as far back as Abraham.

These points are unequivocal, where it establishes that by accepting Christ and *belief* in Him, we are redeemed. Again, I refer to Hebrews 11:6–7. It says, "And without *Faith* it is impossible to please God, because anyone who comes to him must *believe* that he exists, and that he rewards those who earnestly seek him." For example, he says in Hebrews 11:7, "By *faith* Noah, when warned about things not yet seen, in holy fear, built an Ark to save his family. By his *faith* he condemned the world and became an heir of the righteousness that is in keeping with *Faith*."

Our hopes and dreams are fulfilled in our *Faith*. Our *Faith* is our title deed. I have heard God's word, and I believed, and my *Faith* is my title deed to my salvation, to my righteousness, of which I received by my *Faith* in Jesus Christ and in His righteousness, not my own but His, Christ's, performance on the way and at the Cross and my *belief* in that and those facts alone. This is what makes one righteous. We are made righteous in His, Christ's, righteousness and the finished work of the cross, and by this determination, I am the righteousness of Almighty God in Jesus Christ, just as everyone who *believes* in the true gospel of Jesus Christ, His *Grace*, and to whom this has been revealed.

As my pastor and teacher Joseph Prince says, "Right *believing* leads to right thinking." As it has been revealed for us to be able to receive by this *Faith* in the one whom God sent to be His propitiatory sacrifice and to redeem all of us back to God by His sacrificial and most righteous act, punishing sin and also conquering over death and declaring that "It is finished," *redeeming all who believe* and call on His name.

In this current time that we are in, we live in a fallen and sinful world. Since the disobedience of Adam in the garden of Eden. Most of the Old Testament is prophecy and history. And again, I suggest His story, and a documentary of the Jewish people's path, as well as, primarily, a forerunner and prototype of picture messages of the coming Messiah. In many of the Old Testament stories that foretell and predict in specific detail our coming savior, a good example of that is most of the book of Isaiah, which was written approximately eight hundred years before the Messiah's arrival, and it predicts in the most specific of details of the Messiah, our Savior Jesus Christ's coming, laying down of His life for our redemption, His death on the cross and resurrection, His deity, which He laid down while He was God the Son, yielding our reconciliation back to the Father. In fact, that is what most of the book of Isaiah is, almost completely messianic in its nature. For example, in Isaiah 43, it is captioned as Israel's only Savior, and I must admit it is very profound. Isaiah 43:1–7 says:

> But now, this is what the LORD says—he who created you, Jacob, he who formed you, Israel: "do not fear, for I have redeemed you; I have summoned you by name; you are mine. When you pass through the waters, I will be with you. And when you pass through the rivers, they will not sweep over you; when you walk through the fire, you will not be burned for the flames will not set you ablaze. For I am the LORD your God, the Holy one of Israel, your Savior; I give Egypt for your ransom, Cush and Sheba in your stead. Since you are precious and honored in my sight, and because I love you, I will give people in exchange for you, nations in exchange for your life. Do not be afraid, for I am with you; I will bring your children from the east and gather you from the West. I will say to the north, "Give them up!" And to the south, do not hold them back!" Bring my sons from a far and my daughters from the ends of the earth—everyone who is called by my name, whom I created for my glory, whom I formed and made.

Paul receives advanced teachings

In Galatians, there is a good deal of information into the inner workings of the disciples and Paul and Barnabas. Paul's writings are some of the most insightful and advanced revelations that came after the resurrection of Jesus after he had his road to Damascus experience. Being blinded by the brightness and the glory of the risen Christ, which happened when the risen Christ appeared before him, the brightness and glory burned his eyes to a point of scabbing that blinded him for three days until the Holy Spirit calls to Anannais (which means the *Grace* of God) in a vision to go to Paul and heal him. Not to be lost or missed is that Saul, who would become Paul, was an avid persecutor of the disciples, causing very much strife and difficulty for them and was present and supported the stoning to death of Stephen.

Then God begins the conversion, revelation, and teaching to Paul, literally casting him anew and changing his name from Saul to Paul, revealing to him over time all the things that are in the books of the Bible that he penned, which we believe to be from Romans to Hebrews and everything in between. It has been asserted that the Holy Spirit spent up to and as much as three years reforming, retraining, and preparing and revealing all things to Paul. Thus, they are termed the "Pauline" writings because of the unity of style and language and the course they followed according to God's calling on Paul. I would like to assert here, if it has not been already disclosed, that the most loving, caring, and spiritual woman in my life was my grandmother, and she was named Pauline. That, my friends, is no coincidence.

Galatians 2:1–10 begins with Paul and Barnabas returning to Jerusalem after fourteen years and having a gathering with the disciples.

> Then after 14 years, I went up again to Jerusalem, this time with Barnabas. I took Titus along also. I went in response to a revelation and, meeting privately with those esteemed as leaders, I presented to them the gospel that I preach among the Gentiles. I wanted to be sure I was not running, and had not been running, my race in vain. Yet, not even Titus, who was with me was compelled to be circumcised, even though he was a Greek. This matter arose because some false believers

had infiltrated our ranks to spy on the freedom we have in Christ Jesus, and to make us slaves. We did not give in to them for a moment, so that the truth of the gospel might be preserved for you. As for those who were held in high esteem—whatever they were makes no difference to me; God does not show favoritism—they added nothing to my message. On the contrary, they recognized that I had been entrusted with the task of preaching the Gospel to the uncircumcised, (Gentiles or non-Jews), just as Peter had been to the circumcised (Hebrews). For God, who was at work in Peter as an apostle to the circumcised, was also at work in me as an apostle to the Gentiles. James, Cephas, and John, those esteemed pillars, gave me and Barnabas the right hand of fellowship. When they recognized the *Grace* given to me. They agree that we should go to the Gentiles, and they, to the circumcised. All they asked was that we should continue to remember the poor, the very thing I had been eager to do all along.

There are assertions and many in error in the body of many churches today. I have over the years been exposed to many different interpretations and takes on the New Testament. And prior to my revelation of understanding that has broken through over the last two to three years, I have, through much study, been able to weed out many of the doctrinal errors and misteachings that plague today's churches. One of which is primarily the relevancy of Paul and his revelations that were given to him by the Holy Spirit after his road to Damascus moment where he was reformed from being a persecutor of the Christians and of the church of Jesus Christ into being its newest, most radical and zealous-filled apostle of the words of Jesus Christ that we have known.

I have even heard the writings of Paul referred to as "crazy teachings" and even much worse. I can tell you this, there could not be anything any further from the accuracy of the truth than the demeaning, minimizing, or discrediting the intense writings of the Apostle Paul. For even just above in the last quoted scripture given from Galatians 2:1–10, it clearly assesses and asserts the validity, accuracy, and emphatic magnanimity that his writings contain.

Furthermore, in the above-referenced scripture, it clearly states that as Paul met, discussed, and shared his revelations from the Holy Spirit with them that it became clearer as the scriptures say that they added nothing to the doctrine he was teaching but that he had added a "truckload" (a Les Feldick quote) to them and their understanding. As you can see from that scripture of Galatians 2:1–10, they all agreed and shook hands upon the fact that Paul's new instructions and teaching were intended for the Gentiles or the uncircumcised and that Peter and the rest of the twelve would preach only to the circumcised or the Hebrews in Jerusalem and in the surrounding countryside.

I would like to continue to develop this theme here just a little bit further and visit the epistles that Peter wrote, wherein he refers to this very subject. In 2 Peter 3:15–16, it says:

> Bear in mind that our Lord's patience means salvation, just as our dear brother Paul also wrote you with the wisdom that God gave him. he writes the same way in all his letters, speaking in them of these matters. His letters contain some things that are hard to understand, which ignorant and unstable people distort, as they do the other Scriptures, to their own destruction.

For what is divulged in this scripture is that Peter here is admitting that the teaching that Paul has been preaching, given to him of the Holy Spirit, is more advanced, deeper, and more challenging for even Peter, one of the apostles, to grasp. As was stated before in this meeting of Paul and the rest of the apostles. It is beyond clear. As said above, they added nothing to his gospel, where that was just simply not the case with what he added to them and theirs.

THERE IS A DOORWAY...

For Paul's newer version of the plan for salvation was not taught to or by the apostles until it was revealed by Jesus Christ to Paul because the majority of the Hebrew or Jewish people refused to believe or accept it of which God foreknew they would not after the stoning to death of the apostle Stephen, which Paul had witnessed and even held the coats of the participants and cheered them on approvingly.

I am also firmly convinced, after much study and contemplation, that from the very depths of Paul's soul, he was woefully ashamed of his previous behavior in the persecution of the church of Jesus Christ and His apostles. It is as much as verified in his dedication, perseverance, and tribulation that he endured for the rest of his life, even unto the very giving of that life for the word of God, as it was taught to him by the Son Christ Jesus, risen after his road to Damascus experience of conversion as He appeared to him. Following along with the storyline of Paul, in Acts, we find out that after Anannais, which is "Hannahniah" in Hebrew and means "the *Grace* of God," was called by the Holy Spirit to go to Paul and lay hands on him and cure him of his blindness.

So it is certainly no coincidence that the first thing Paul sees when he opens his restored eyes is a man with a name that means "the *Grace* of God." Remember, there are no insignificant details in the Bible; it is unequivocally the inspired, breathed, Holy Word of God. Our God is so amazing, powerful, just, and clever! It is then mentioned that Paul, whose name was Saul, went to the mountains of Arabia where he stayed for possibly two to three years. Not said specifically, but it is inferred, that this is the time where the Holy Spirit of the risen Christ met, taught, and mentored Paul to prepare him for the commission God would entrust him with—the taking of God's word and salvation plan to redeem all mankind, namely the Gentile world, as was Paul's special assignment from God. Nowhere could this be more clearly asserted than in the verses here. I will quote here Romans 3:20–26:

> Therefore no one will be declared righteous
> in God's sight by the works of the Law; rather,

through the Law we become conscious of our sin. But now apart from the Law, the righteousness of God has been made known, to which the Law and the prophets testify. This righteousness is given through Faith in Jesus Christ to all who *believe*. There is no difference between Jew and Gentile, for all have sinned and fall far short of the glory of God, and all are justified freely by his Grace through the redemption that came by Christ Jesus. God presented Christ as a sacrifice of atonement, through the shedding of his blood—to be received by Faith. He did this to demonstrate his righteousness, because in his forbearance he had left the sins committed beforehand unpunished—he did it to demonstrate his righteousness at the present time, so-as-to be Just, and the one who justifies those who have Faith in Jesus.

It is a primary plank in God's plan of salvation and in His divine righteousness and justice that "without the shedding of Blood, there can be no remission of Sin." This elemental stand that God has declared in His righteousness and delivery of this present system of things is integral to the understanding of God's word, His Salvation plan for us, and our complete reality in this existence, as well as instituting it in the Mosaic Law issued through Moses after the deliverance of the Hebrew people from Egypt.

It is in the very mechanization and exacting specifics of this revealing that confirm, elucidate, and reveal just who and how loving our God is that we are blessed to have the interworking and multiplicity of layers of the Bible and the gospel of Jesus Christ that reveal God's heart for us, His wisdom and majesty, and give us a glimpse of what is His glory, amen, of which I am one of the fortunate that He has chosen to reveal and give understanding to, by His *Grace*.

The book of Acts is widely recognized as having been written by the disciple Luke, the physician. In Acts 10, Luke records the words of Peter, who was sent to the centurion Cornelius's house. Cornelius was a Gentile who also was a *believer* in Christ. He and his family were devout *believers* and God-fearing who gave generously to those in need and prayed to God regularly. One day, while praying, the angel of the Lord answered, as recorded in Acts 10, starting in verse 3:

> One day at about three in the afternoon he had a vision. He distinctly saw an Angel of God, who came to him and said "Cornelius!" Cornelius stared at him in fear. What is it Lord? He asked. The Angel answered, your prayers and gifts to the poor have come up as a memorial offering before God. Now send men to Joppa to bring back a man named Simon, who is called Peter. He is staying with Simon the tanner who houses by the sea. When the Angels spoke to him had gone, Cornelius called two of his servants and the devout soldier who was one of his attendants. He told them everything that had happened and sent them to Joppa. about noon the following day as they were on their journey and are approaching the city, Peter went up on the roof to pray. He became hungry and wanted something to eat, and while the meal was being prepared, he fell into a trance. He saw heaven opened in something like a large sheet being let down to the earth by its four corners. It contained all kinds of four-footed animals, as well as reptiles and birds. Then a voice told him, "Get up, Peter. Kill and eat." "Surely not Lord!" Peter replied. "I have never eaten anything impure or unclean." The voice spoke to him a second time, "Do not call anything impure that God has made clean." This happened three times, and immediately the sheet was taken back to heaven. while Peter was wondering about the meaning of the vision, the

man sent by Cornelius found out where Simon's house was and stopped at the gate. they called out, asking if Simon who was known as Peter was staying there. while Peter was still thinking about the vision, the Spirit said to him, "Simon, three men are looking for you. So get up and go downstairs. Do not hesitate to go with them, for I have sent them." Peter went down and said to the man, "I am the one you're looking for. Why have you come?" the man replied, "We have come from Cornelius the Centurion. He is a righteous and God-fearing man, who is respected by all the Jewish people. A holy angel told him to ask you to come to his house so that he could hear what you have to say." Then Peter invited, the man into the house to be his guests. The next day Peter started out with them, and some of the *believers* from Joppa went along. the following day he arrived in Caesarea. Cornelius was expecting them and had called together his relatives and close friends. As Peter entered the house, Cornelius met him and fell at his feet in reverence. But Peter made him get up. "Stand up", he said, "I am only a man myself." While talking with him, Peter went inside and found a large gathering of people. he said to them: "You are aware that it is against our law for a Jew to associate with or visit a Gentile. But God has shown me that I should not call anyone impure or unclean. So when I was sent for, I came without raising any objection. May I ask why you sent for me?" Cornelius answered: "Three days ago I was in my house praying at this hour, at three in the afternoon. Suddenly a man in shining clothes stood before me, and said, "Cornelius, God has heard your prayer and remembered your gifts to the poor. Send to Joppa

> for Simon, who is called Peter. He is a guest in the house of Simon the tanner, who lives by the sea." So I sent for you immediately, and it was good of you to come. Now we are all here in the presence of God to listen to everything the Lord has commanded you to tell us.

I will break here temporarily and explain that all the last large paragraphs of scripture were chosen specifically to set up and introduce information that is getting ready to be released as Peter speaks to this gathering of Gentile believers, non-Jewish or non-Hebrew people, because of the new dispensation that has been released at the cross by Christ Jesus and is now being taught by the Holy Spirit to Paul first and then to the rest of the disciples, namely Peter, here. Now we will pick back up, continuing in Acts 10, as Peter addresses the crowd with what is a very powerful few paragraphs of an encapsulated version, dynamically putting the salvation plan and the gospel, as had been prophesied for 1,500 years. Here we go…

> Then Peter began to speak: "I now realize how true it is that God does not show favoritism, but accepts from every nation, the one who fears him and does what is right. You know, the message God sent to the people of Israel, announcing the good news of peace through Jesus Christ, who is Lord of all. You know, what has happened throughout the province of Judea, beginning in Galilee after the baptism that John preached— How God anointed Jesus of Nazareth with the Holy Spirit and power, and how he went around doing good and healing all who were under the power of the devil, because God was with him. "We are witnesses of everything he did in the country of the Jews and in Jerusalem. They killed Him by hanging Him on the cross, but God raised him from the dead on the third day

and caused him to be seen. He was not seen by all the people, but by witnesses whom God had already chosen—by us, who ate and drank with him after he rose from the dead. He commanded us to preach to the people and to testify that he is the one whom God appointed as judge of the living and the dead. All the prophets testify about him that everyone who *believes* in him receives forgiveness of sins through his name." While Peter was still speaking these words, the Holy Spirit came on all who heard the message. The circumcised *believers* who had come with Peter were astonished that the gift of the Holy Spirit had been poured out even on Gentiles. For they heard them speaking in tongues and praising God. Then Peter said, "Surely no one can stand in the way of their being baptized with water. They have received the Holy Spirit, just as we have. So he ordered that they be baptized in the name of Jesus Christ. Then they asked Peter to stay with them for a few days."

These words spoken by Peter to the centurion Cornelius and his family and friends and followers similarly aligned with the revelation that was given to Paul by Holy Spirit in his assignment to take the Gospel of *Grace* to the Gentile world or everyone outside of the Hebrew people, in the rest of the world, this was the eventuality that resulted from the rejection and the denial of Jesus Christ by the Jewish population and majority of the Hebrew people. It was in this failure of Israel to receive the Messiah, His message and kingdom, that deliver the eventual plan of salvation that was released to the Gentiles, through the Gospel of Grace by Jesus Christ upon His crucifixion at the Cross on Calvary. The following two scriptures are added here in the confirmation of the assertions established in the last group of scriptures. One is from the Old Testament. One is from the New Testament. As we know, the majority of the book of Isaiah is messianic in its nature as this verse supports clearly.

> After he has suffered, he will see the light of life and be satisfied; By his knowledge, my righteous servant will justify many, and he will bear their iniquities. Therefore I will give him a portion among the great, and he will divide the spoils with the strong, because he poured out his life unto death, and was numbered with the transgressors. For he bore the sin of many and made intercession for the transgressors. (Isaiah 53:11–12)

This scripture verse well speaks for itself, as will the next scripture in referencing this subject found in John 1 verse 11, which states, "He came to that which was his own, but his own did not receive him." We must remember that this messianic scripture written in Isaiah was declared in this prophecy, approximately eight hundred years prior to the Messiah Jesus Christ's appearance as well as most of the other chapters. For in God's foreknowledge and wisdom and justice, He has been overtly and covertly calling and declaring His divine righteousness to all His children since the very beginning of our existence in His eternal and divine *Grace* for us to receive Him through the Messiah's righteousness that He has worked out before us, freely offered from the beginning to receivers of the Word and those *believing* in it, like Abraham, not performing or establishing our righteousness, which we have none, but resting in our *belief* in Jesus Christ, the finished work of the Cross, the resurrection, our Father God, and the Holy Spirit. God Almighty. El Shaddai.

In Romans, the first chapter that is penned by Paul is the beginning of what is labeled as the Pauline doctrine and in my opinion is where we begin to gain traction in unboxing the dynamite of God's word, the new message of the Gospel of Grace and entry into our God's eternal family by belief in the Son and the work of the Cross. Although the doctrine of the establishment of God's Grace is initiated first in the garden, then with Abraham, the patriarch of the Hebrew people, it is not fully defined to the level of clarity and complexity that Paul's epistles do reveal about this Gospel of the *Grace* and Truth of Jesus Christ and specifically God's *Grace* other than this reference from Romans 4:3, "Abraham *believed* the things that God told him, and it was counted unto him as righteousness," as it says in Genesis. (Righteousness by *Faith*, yes, in the Old Testament!) For the meaning that is behind this concept of Grace is much deeper than what is inferred by the surface definition, which merely suggests that this, God's Grace, is similar to just a good blessing. I will strongly suggest that it is much more than that.

The Grace of God is the very power of God—everything that is good, for He is completely righteous and pure intelligence. The currency that unlocks this mighty power of God's *Grace* is our *Faith* in His Son Jesus Christ and the Father from whom He was sent. Amen. In 2 Corinthians 12:7–10, it says of this *Grace*,

> Therefore, in order to keep me from becoming conceited, I was given a thorn in my flesh, a messenger of Satan, to torment me. Three times. I pleaded with the Lord to take it away from me. But He said to me, "My *Grace* is sufficient for you, for my power is made perfect in weakness. Therefore, I will boast all-the-more gladly about my weaknesses, so that Christ's power may rest on me. That is why, for Christ's sake, I delight in weaknesses, in the insults, in hardships, in persecutions, in difficulties. For when I am weak, then I am strong.

And I will only add here His perfection, majesty, and the Grace of His love abounds to us, and for us, through our weaknesses, our sins, and our awareness of our need for our Savior. This Grace is the evidence of the love of God, revealing His heart to us, revealed through the Son and His decision to not spare Him but pay the "ransom" for us to redeem us into the ultimate intended God family now and for eternity. This Grace is better and more accurately defined as, "the unmerited favor or undeserved kindness or, even yet, the mercy and divine love God has for us."

This merging of the Hebrew people, God's chosen people, or vehicle that brought us the Messiah was intended by God, with His foreknowledge of their stubbornness and how they would reject Him, that the Gospel of the Grace and Truth of Jesus Christ would go to the rest of the world. Eventually, after His second coming, which is affirmed by much Bible prophecy, He will graft the two groups of sheep into one flock, with the good shepherd for all of eternity, which is ultimately what this has all been for and about. Jesus Christ affirms this to us in John 10:11–18:

> I am the good shepherd. The good Shepherd lays down his life for the sheep. The hired hand is not the Shepherd and does not own the sheep. So, when he sees the wolf coming, he abandons the sheep and runs away. Then the wolf attacks the flock and scatters it. The man runs away because he is a hired hand and cares nothing for the sheep. I am the good Shepherd; I know my sheep and my sheep know me—Just as the father knows me and I know the father—and I lay down my life for the sheep. I have other sheep that are not of this sheep pen. I must bring them also. They too will listen to my voice, and there shall be one flock and one Shepherd. The reason, my father loves me is that I lay down my life—only to take it up again. No one takes it from me, but I lay it down of my own accord. I have authority to lay it down and authority to take it up again. This command I received from my father.

Yes, this book is directing you to God, Jehovah, to help us, me, and you unlock the mysteries of this universe as God almighty, the "El Shaddai," has revealed them to us all by His Holy Spirit, as He promises in His word to us, the Holy Bible, that He would and will do!

There is a planned progression in the evolving story of the Bible, where the Old Testament delivers and evolves into the new. As I have stated previously, these terms would be better and more accurately rendered as old covenant and new covenant. Nonetheless, the evolution and transference of God's *Grace* and protection over His people are chronicled in the Holy Scriptures. One of the best examples that totally epitomizes this transference and delivery of the old Mosaic Law given to bind the people to God, Jehovah, of the Old Testament, was replaced by Jesus Christ and His finished work on the Cross.

God's only begotten son, Jesus Christ the Messiah, has been prophesied through His own people to come for nearly 1,500 years in the oral traditions and recorded scrolls alike, given in exchange for the redemption of all who choose to *believe* in Him, as the will of God commands. For in John 6:40, it reads, "For my father's will is that everyone who looks to the son and *believes* in him shall have eternal life, and I will raise them up at the last day."

Now to continue with the example I was citing previously that delineates explicitly God's newly established covenant of Grace through His Son Jesus Christ and the finished work at Calvary on the Cross, this event is referred to and is most commonly called the Transfiguration, which I've lightly referred to in previous chapters, and is one of the words defined in the glossary. This transfiguration is spoken of in Luke 9, beginning in verse 28. I will put the verses first, then extrapolate, and glean out the meaning thereafter. Luke 9:28–35 says:

> About eight days after Jesus said this, he took Peter, John and James with him and went up onto a mountain to pray. As he was praying, the appearance of his face changed, and his clothes became bright as a flash of lightning. Two men, Moses and Elijah, appeared in glorious splendor, talking with Jesus. They spoke about his departure, which he was to about to bring

to fulfillment at Jerusalem. Peter and his companions were very sleepy, but when they became fully awake, they saw his glory and the two men standing with him. As the men were leaving Jesus, Peter said to him, Master is it good for us to be here? Let us put up three shelters—one for you, one for Moses and one for you Elijah." (He did not know what he was saying.) While he was speaking, a cloud appeared and covered them, and they were afraid as they entered the cloud. a voice came from the clouds, saying, this is my son, whom I have chosen; listen to him." When the voice had spoken, they found that Jesus was alone. The disciples kept this to themselves and did not tell anyone at that time, what they had seen.

Critical in the breakdown of this story are the names of the three disciples that Jesus took with him and, equally, names of the two that appeared with Jesus on the Mount of Transfiguration, where His glory shone and His appearance was changed before their eyes, and in their bewilderment, they were mystified, confused, and were very sleepy as given in the reading of these passages.

As Peter becomes semicoherent for a moment or two, he even inquires of Jesus. If they should be there, and that to properly accommodate the glory, they should build a temporary tabernacle booth or shelter to contain such brilliance and glory of the Lord, which was before them. Inherent in the message contained in these passages of the reference are the two men that appeared with Jesus as He was being transfigured before the disciples. The Bible tells us it was Moses and Elijah that were with Jesus, with Moses representing the Law and Elijah the prophets. It is when Peter asks Jesus first if it was good for them to be there. Secondly, should not he build three temporary shelters for the three: Jesus, Moses, and Elijah (confirming Jesus by the Law and the Prophets).

At this, the Heavenly Father speaks from the cloud that was hovering over them and says, "This is my son, whom I have chosen; listen to him." It says just after that, once the voice had finished speaking from the cloud, the two men left, and Jesus was alone before the three disciples. Huge in the meaning of these scriptures is the fact that the name Peter means stone, James means to supplant or replace, and John is the Grace of God and is God's direct command to all present before them that they should listen to Him, Jesus, alone and not the two men, Moses and Elijah, and that their day had passed and a new dispensation was being delivered by Christ Jesus, and that was the establishment of God's Law of Grace by Faith in Jesus Christ and the Cross.

For that was the inferred meaning by the three disciples in their names that Christ took with Him to the Transfiguration and was verified by the word of God that came out of the clouds when He said for them to hear His son. Reinforcing this is the meaning in the names of the disciples that were with them. The Law is written on stone represented by Peter, is supplanted or replaced represented by James, with God's Law of Grace symbolized by the name John, and in Hebrew, it means Jehovah, or Jah, has been gracious.

So in conjunction, the two major themes of these passages both reinforce the message from the Father that the old Law by the finished work of Jesus Christ on the Cross that has been fulfilled and replaced in the Law of Grace, which delivers to us our redemption and salvation plan with which we receive sonship with the Father, citizenship in the kingdom, and the position of priesthood in the family of God. It says in 2 Corinthians 5:21, "God made him who had no sin to be sin for us, so that in him we might become the righteousness of God." Our salvation transcends this reality and is a gift to us from the divine. It is a complete and simple beauty. For Jesus Christ Himself is the very embodiment of God's *Grace*, as He was given in exchange for us children of Abraham, who have *Faith* in God's Word, and is also why it has been hidden from the wise and the prudent. In God's wisdom, "his *belief* in what God has said" was accounted to Him as righteousness. This is exactly how our salvation resides in our *Faith* in Him, Yeshua or Jesus, which avails us our righteous standing before God. Not wise, righteous. Amen.

THERE IS A DOORWAY...

For we are directed once we have our minds opened up to the Law of Grace to be received by our belief in Jesus Christ and the finished work of the Cross that we do not look at our Faith; we look at Jesus. For if you look at your Faith, it can fly away. But look at Jesus Christ, and your Faith will surely stay. The Bible says the Law was given by Moses, but Grace and Peace and Truth came by Jesus Christ the son of the living God, God in human flesh. It takes the son to unfold and explain the very heart of God. For as it says in Colossians 1:15–20:

> The son is the image of the invisible God, the firstborn over all creation. For in Him all things were created: things in heaven and on earth, visible and invisible, whether thrones or powers or rulers or authorities; all things have been created through him and for him. He is before all things, and in Him all things hold together. and he is the head of the body, the church; he is the beginning and the firstborn from among the dead. So that in everything he might have supremacy. For God was pleased to have all his fullness dwell in him, and through Him to reconcile to Himself all things, whether things on earth or things in heaven, by making peace through His blood, shed on the Cross.

Unless we accept and receive the new covenant, established at the Cross by Christ, containing the Law of Grace, we cannot receive our inheritance in the here and now. It is in His *Grace* God wants us to approach Him, in our *belief* or *faith*, without consciousness of our sin, *believing* that our righteousness, which means simply we have been made right with God, cannot be received or achieved by our own performance. We receive His righteousness by accepting and *believing* in Jesus Christ. His Grace is given to us by Faith in Him. And thus, it removes our awareness of a sin debt that He has already paid upon our acceptance and belief in that only, leaving for us to receive His supply of Grace and love, through our *Faith* in Jesus.

We have acquired by the gift of God our sanctification and our righteous standing before God. For through Christ's sacrifice and our acceptance and *belief* in that, we are washed clean by His holy blood that was shed for us. For He who knew no sin, who did no sin, and whom in Him there was no sin became sin and took our place of condemnation, paying the price for us who had done no right thing, so that we may become the righteousness of God by our *belief* in His holiness and sacrifice. Amen.

We get this not of our own merit; it is freely given to all who will receive it, and through this gift, by which we accept and *believe* in the Son of God whom the Father sent on our behalf, these elements have all been put in place by the love and desire of our Father God, Jehovah, who is establishing through Christ, the firstborn of all creation, an eternal family, as we will be a part of now and into eternity. And it is from this gift that we have received by our *belief* that delivers our righteous standing before God, which is yielded and delivered to us *believers* through the just and righteous acts of the Father through the Son. In Hebrews 3:1–6, it speaks directly to this:

> Therefore, holy brothers and sisters, who share in the heavenly calling, fix your thoughts on Jesus, whom we acknowledge as our apostle and high priest. He was *faithful* to the one who appointed him, just as Moses was *faithful* in all God's house. Jesus has been found worthy of a greater honor than Moses, just as the builder of a house has greater honor than the house itself. for every house is built by someone, but God is the builder of everything. "Moses was *faithful* as a servant in all God's house", bearing witness to what would be spoken by God in the future. But Christ is *faithful* as the Son over God's house. And we are his house, if indeed we hold firmly to our confidence and the hope in which we glory.

THERE IS A DOORWAY…

And another scripture which speaks well to this follows here, from Hebrews also, in chapter 1:1–4:

> In the past, God spoke to our ancestors through the prophets at many times and in many various ways, but in these last days he has spoken to us by his son, whom he appointed heir of all things, and through whom also he made the universe. The son is the radiance of God's glory and the exact representation of his being, sustaining all things by his powerful Word. After he had provided purification for sins, He sat down at the right hand of the Majesty in heaven. So he became much superior to the Angels, as the name he inherited is superior to theirs.

This gift then of our salvation, and our righteous standing before God is purely a gift received by our *belief* in Jesus Christ and the finished work at the Cross and not from our performing any work, upholding any law, or any legalist requirement, other than our acceptance by *believing* and our ability to receive God's love, *Grace*, salvation, and redemption through the son and our *believing* in the words of Him and the Father.

His *Grace* was given to us at the Cross, for He is *Grace* personified and removes the sin debt of all who truly *believe*. For I now am the righteousness of Almighty God in Jesus Christ. This *Grace* of God produces true holiness, for *Grace* gives and distributes God's gifts. And these are the fruits of the Spirit, which are nicely expounded upon in 1 Corinthians 12:1–11:

> Now about the gifts of the Spirit, brothers and sisters, I do not want you to be uninformed. You know that when you were pagans, somehow or other you were influenced and led astray by mute idols. Therefore, I want you to know that no one who is speaking by the Spirit of God

says. Jesus be cursed, and no one can say Jesus is Lord, except by the Holy Spirit. There are different kinds of gifts, but the same Spirit distributes them. There are different kinds of service, but the same Lord. There are different kinds of working, but in all of them, and in everyone it is the same God at work. Now to each one the manifestation of the Spirit is given for the common good. To one there is given through the Spirit a message of wisdom, to another a message of knowledge by means of the same spirit, to another *faith*, by means of the same spirit, to another gifts of healing by that one Spirit, to another miraculous powers, to another prophecy, to another distinguishing between spirits, to another speaking in different kinds of tongues, and to still another, the interpretation of tongues. All these are the work of one and the same spirit, and he distributes them to each one, just as he determines.

Continuing on with just how powerful the Law of *Grace* that was revealed by Christ at the Cross is, and shed for us by His life and His blood, coupled with our *belief* in those facts, born out in Bible scripture—our righteous savior—by redeeming us and establishing our salvation and our righteous standing before God. There is another scripture that reads, "The fervent and effective prayer of a righteous man avails much." The chapter and verse are not critical here. I am simply going to use this scripture to help illustrate something that confused me previously and of which I now have clarity on.

In error, I initially believed that the righteous man referred to in this scripture spoke completely of something other than what it is. For in my misunderstanding, I assumed this righteous man was righteous by his performance or standing in the community or of some form of qualification or special requirement that one could obtain or possess, more than likely, in my assumption, by deeds or works or some achieved or derived status. However, the New Covenant of Jesus Christ, His "Law of Grace," sets all this straight. For these righteous men are you and me and all *believers* that call on the name of our Lord and Savior Jesus Christ.

We have this righteous standing before God due to our *faith* in Jesus Christ and through His released "Law of Grace" within which we benefit from the divine exchange, where the Almighty God gave Christ in exchange for all the sin in the world of those who choose to *believe* in the Son whom He sent, Jesus Christ our Lord. Our prayers are heard by God because of Jesus's atoning sacrifice on the Cross. We are washed in Jesus's blood when we *believe* in Him, which yields our righteous standing before God, as we have been washed and are spotless before God by that most holy blood shed at the Cross at Calvary. As the Bible says, "The just shall live by faith." As Christ's righteousness is transferred to us by our *Faith* in Him, justified.

It was by Almighty God's divine righteousness and justice that established with Israel in the Old Testament and the Pentateuch, or the first five books penned by Moses of the Old Testament, that declared and established God's requirement that without the shedding of blood, there can be no remission of sin. This was fulfilled in the keeping of the Law by the Hebrews up until the death of Christ and was fulfilled as predicted by the coming of the Messiah, Jesus Christ, who gave Himself as a ransom for the many in keeping with God's established justice, righteousness, and divine plan, which yields to us by the price paid by God Himself for our salvation and redemption by the atoning sacrifice of Christ, whom God has chosen and conducted for the purpose of establishing us back into the presence of God, through Jesus Christ, which ultimately will graft together both Jews and Gentiles into one people for all eternity, where He will be our king and father God where He will truly be an *Immanuel*, which means "God who is with us."

In Hebrews 4:16, it says, "Let us then approach God's throne of *Grace* with confidence. So that we may receive mercy and find Grace to help us in our time of need." It is directly referring here the knowledge and awareness of our sin debt or the misperception that we are or have been alienated from God and live with a guilt consciousness that continually works for the enemy as an impediment to us in gaining, receiving, and living in communion with the Father, which has been made available to us by the plan of our salvation and redemption. That is so freely offered from God the Father to be received by the accepting and the *believing* in the Son, the chosen one of Israel, the Messiah, Jesus Christ, the one whom the Father sent.

Many people are stumbled here, as much as in any other place, for it is one of the many devices of the enemy to confuse us with wrong teachings, which reinforce wrong *believing*, as one of my teachers, Singapore's Pastor Joseph Prince, whom I have been studying under for the last several years, has helped make it more clear to me, as he espouses directly from the Bible, God's Word. I am going to develop this out a little further here. So then, given our previous state of confusion in the knowledge of God and His true gospel, it would then be difficult for us to approach God's throne with competence and confidence until we have experienced a change of mind or repentance so that we are able to allow God through His Holy Spirit to open our minds to these new and fresh concepts that establish that we are not guilty any longer and that Jesus Christ has paid our sin debt in full and even *overabundantly* at the cross.

We are washed clean by Christ's blood shed on the cross by the spotless lamb—the ransom of the *divine one* that was paid as an exchange for the sins of the many. It is paramount that we must receive this new truth about the Grace and Truth of Jesus Christ (God), revealed in His ministry and expounded heavily upon by Paul in most of His epistles. But for now, I will reference a scripture found in 1 John 4:13–21, which dovetails nicely with the concept we are establishing here.

> This is how we know that we live in him and he in us: he has given us up his spirit. And we have seen and testified that the father has sent his son to be the savior of the world. If anyone that acknowledges that Jesus is the son of God, God lives in them and they in God. And so we know and rely on the love God has for us. God

> is love. Whoever lives in love lives in God, and God in them. This is how love is made complete among us so that we will have confidence on the day of judgment: In this world we are like Jesus. There is no fear in love. But perfect love, drives-out fear, because fear has to do with punishment. The one who fears is not made perfect in love. We love because he first loved us. Whoever claims to love God yet hates a brother or sister is a liar. For whoever does not love their brother and sister, who they have seen, cannot love God, whom they have not seen. And he has given us this command: Anyone who loves God must also love their brother and sister.

Wow, God says it in His word better than I can. Nevertheless, with many people, this is a major mind shift. I know it truly was for me. I had much of the puzzle pieces needed but not them all. This teaching on the Grace of Almighty God displayed through His Son Jesus Christ and in all actuality throughout every page of the Bible were for me those most needed, and the remaining, missing, or misconstrued pieces that needed to be found or shown to me to fall into place as they now have and have thus yielded a clarity of knowledge and power and the zeal that my mind is barely able to contain. All glory and majesty to the Father.

For that is what Jesus Christ came to do—redeem us and glorify His Father and establish our eternal heavenly family. So it was extremely important here to concretely establish some of the engine, or force, that is behind the *Grace* of God. For it is fueled by God's love for us. It also says in John, "For though we were yet sinners Christ first loved us." Hearing this, I began immediately to establish it in my mind. It started to eliminate the cloudiness and establish clarity of these acts that I had been studying and the word of God that had been performed through His prophets, the Messiah, the apostles, and all the stories documented in the Holy Scriptures.

Once this *force* of God's love—yes, His radical love, radical sacrifice, the salvation, and redemption plan—was fully revealed to me, then it finally made sense. *Grace*. For the Scriptures also say that once you find the truth, "the truth will set you free," "and once you've been set free, you will be freed indeed." And I, my friends, have been freed, and I am free indeed in this knowledge and truth of the Law of the Grace and Truth of the Gospel of Jesus Christ.

I am going to continue to further expound on this concept of the New Covenant Law delivered at the Cross, releasing God's loving Grace for all believers. I feel I must continue to define and attempt to explain the power and the glory and majesty of Almighty God that is released in this said *Grace*. For without any shadow of a doubt, for me, it is what most single-handedly changed everything. This knowledge and information, once I received it, then allowed all the other pieces that before had not added up and made sense in the previously mentioned venues where I had been taught.

More conclusively, until I was able to receive and digest the radical love that is divulged in the examination of this *Grace*, I had previously in error, bought into the misinformation that my salvation was contingent upon some performance of my own or my obedience to the Ten Commandments or some form of legalist or performance-based biblical application by which we had to earn our salvation. Nothing could be more further from the truth.

Until I completely digested and began to understand the radical love that is revealed and released from God for us at the Cross by Christ Jesus, even though we were yet sinners. The awareness and the emphasis is placed on God's love for us and that He is not mad at us—quite the opposite, in fact—reversing all the erroneous teachings and misunderstandings that many teachers had placed before me, condemning me in so many different churches and from other false teachings or that we just simply had not read enough or heard the word enough, as I obviously had not. Nor had the Holy Spirit revealed these things to me up to that point, as it is up to Him, until I had heard and received through the saturation of the word for it to be opened up to me. Simply put, until I was ready to understand that all I had to do to receive the eternal salvation being offered to me by

God, through His Son Jesus Christ, was for me to get out of my own way and follow His way to receive my salvation by *Faith* through God's *Grace* and allow the Good Shepherd to simply carry me.

As I lay all my cares—past, present, and future—at the foot of His Cross; and I rest eternally in love, provision, and Peace of Jesus Christ, Almighty God, or "El Shaddai" and walk in the love of God with Him just as I begin to grasp this Law of Grace that encapsulates the love of God for us and our redemption and our salvation. Yes, the *Grace* and *Love* of God are what unblocked the logjam of false doctrine and misunderstanding that had plagued my development and progression to the full truth of God's word, our Holy Bible—my B-i-b-l-e, yes. That is the *book* for me! There is another parable in the scriptures that delves into the story of the good shepherd, one of many.

It speaks of how He is like no other shepherd, for when He, out of a hundred sheep, were to lose one, He is the good shepherd that will leave the other ninety-nine to go and search for the one lost. It is a very beautiful parable, and I am sure it is one I will be using in the chapter on the good shepherd, but it also applies very nicely here—this one lost sheep that the good shepherd went after and searched for until He found. He then called all his friends and gathered them together to throw a party and celebrate the recovery of the one lost sheep. That is our Father God. That one lost sheep was me.

Without any shadow of a doubt or question in my mind, the good shepherd, my Father God, Jesus Christ, and the Holy Spirit, has been calling after me and watching out for me for certain for my whole life. For as a boy of six and a half years old, and in first grade, I suffered an acute appendectomy. My appendix had swollen and inflamed with toxins and poisons and had ruptured and burst inside my stomach cavity. By the time my parents realized this, I was a very sick young man. I was rushed into the emergency room on Monday morning as my father went to work.

My mom took me to the hospital. It did not take them too long to realize that I was on death's door. They prepped me immediately for surgery, as they knew they had little time to spare. Dr. McNinch, the on-duty surgeon, had his hands full and preceded to perform surgery on me, where they completely removed all the contents of my stomach after opening up a large enough flap to enter in to do that. They then had to go in with a suction machine, or vacuum of some sort, to remove all the gangrene and poison that had set in around and behind my other organs. I remained in a coma for four days.

For three days consecutively, my father came directly from work over an hour away straight to the hospital. For each of the three days, there was no change. I remained in a comatose state. On the fourth day, my father trekked back again after work, directly to the hospital. He made his way up to the children's ward, which was a group room that had about ten beds within which I was being housed in my recovery.

As my dad approached the bed that I have been lying in the previous three days, he realized that the bed was empty and had been made, and I was nowhere in sight. At that moment, one can only imagine the thoughts that were going through his head. As he stood there stunned to say the least, he could not even speak the question that was on his mind as the attending nurse came into the children's ward.

Before he was able to speak, as I am sure he was struggling, he was pointing toward my empty bed at which point the nurse finally realized the gravity of the situation and was pleased to inform him said, "No, no, no, Mr. Johnson, heavens no… Ricky woke up today finally, and he is sitting in his wheelchair down the hall watching the fish swim in the aquarium." My father has told me that story many times, and I clearly received just how traumatic a time it was of nearly losing me to death at such a young age. I cannot help but feel there was some divine intervention not just there but also many other places in my life along the way. As scripture also says in Hebrews 13:2, "Forget not to show Love unto strangers; for thereby, some have entertained angels unaware."

It says in 2 Corinthians 3:4–6:

> Such confidence we have through Christ before God. Not that we are competent in ourselves to claim anything for ourselves, but our competence comes from God. He has made us competent as ministers of a New Covenant—not of the letter but of the spirit: for the letter kills, the spirit gives life.

Being under the Law means being or living in the flesh, which is basically a performance-based salvation plan that was given through Moses. Self-righteousness, as it were, was false righteousness. For the scripture says, "For all sin and fall far short of the Glory of God" and "There is none that go without sin, no not one." Being in the spirit means being in His *Grace*. In 2 Corinthians, it also discusses how the Law of Grace is also called the "ministry of His reconciliation." It's about how we are made righteous from our sin by *faith* for our reconciliation to the *faith* through Jesus Christ. For Adam fell, but Jesus Christ lifts us back up to stand. He has shown us the light of the glory of God in the face of Himself the Messiah Jesus Christ. These concepts are the very basis of our reality, our existence, and all life in the universe as we know it. Unfortunately, many may have never heard or have chosen to dismiss and have for one reason or another likely not even been exposed to the accurate truths of the Bible's teachings.

For now, it appears clearly to be "self-evident" after having had the Holy Scriptures opened up with a few doctrinally based effective teachers to help to sort it all out. Amen! The Bible is clear in its directive in Matthew 10:8.5, "Freely you have received it, so freely you should give," or spread the good news of the Gospel of the *Grace* and Truth of Jesus Christ, the prophesied Messiah, the redeemer of all mankind, and our "*believing* in those facts." One thing I know for sure is this, you cannot keep quiet once the Lord begins working in your life, and this, there is no wiser walk than in the way of the Lord. Another illuminating definition of *Grace* is this. It is an equivalent to, or is also defined as "supplied righteousness." For God Almighty supplies us with His righteousness by our belief in the only begotten son whom He sent. When it comes to death, the only thing we will need is Jesus; nothing else will go with us. For He, Jesus Christ, is our righteousness. I am the righteousness of Almighty God in Christ Jesus and His finished work on the Cross, just as all *believers* in Him, and those facts are. For it states in Matthew 11:27–30:

> All things have been committed to me by my Father. No one knows the Son except the Father, and no one knows the Father except the Son, and those whom the Son chooses to reveal Him. Come to me, all who are weary and burdened, and I will give you rest. Take my yoke upon you and learn from me, for I am gentle and humble in heart, and you will find rest for your souls. For my yoke is easy and my burden is light.

Now excuse me here, but I must state that this does not sound like a demanding, condemning, and ruthless, nonloving, or uncompassionate God. Christ said also in John 6:46, "If you have seen me, you have seen the Father." For our righteousness is attained by our faith in Jesus Christ and His crucifixion, death, burial, and resurrection.

This received righteousness is the primary revelation of the Gospel of Grace and Truth. For Jesus Christ, the Messiah, came representing the Father. For Moses brought the Law, but Grace and Truth came by Jesus Christ. Most people know God is holy. What people need to know about is His radical love for us and His radical *Grace* and that it is released to us by our *Faith* and hope in Christ Jesus. For *Faith* is the currency that flows and moves God. He delivers to all *believers* in Him a peace and calm over us that surpasses all human understanding. After all… He is God. The word declares that unless we reveal to others this *radical love and radical Grace of God*, through His Son Jesus Christ, lives will not be *radically* changed, as Pastor Joseph Prince teaches.

In other very informative writings, Paul expounds on the Holy Spirit, *Grace*, Jesus's divinity, and many other lofty doctrinal concepts. We find in 2 Corinthians that he has been pleading with our Lord and Savior to remove some sort of "thorn in the flesh" issue that sinfully plagues him, and the Lord's reply is quite profound and is here from 2 Corinthians 12:7.5–10:

> Therefore, in order to keep me from becoming conceited, I was given a thorn in my flesh, a Messenger of Satan, to torment me. Three times I pleaded with the Lord to take it away from me. But he said to me, my *Grace* is sufficient for you, for my power is made perfect in weakness. Therefore, I will boast all-the-more gladly about my weaknesses, so that Christ's power may rest on me. That is why, for Christ's sake, I delight in weaknesses, in insults, in hardships, in persecutions, in difficulties, for when I am weak, then I am strong.

That is what He calls us to do—to lay our concerns and burdens at the foot of the Cross so that He may carry them for us. For all things work together for the good purposes of us who love God. Less of us, and more of Jesus in us. For the more we behold the glory of the image of Chirst Jesus, the more we are changed into His likeness.

It says in 2 Corinthians 3:18, cited here to verify for accuracy in the word, "And we all, with *unveiled* faces contemplate the Lord's glory, are being transformed into His image with ever-increasing glory, which comes from the Lord, who is the Spirit." In Galatians 3:11–14, it says:

> Clearly no one who relies on the Law is justified before God, because the righteous will live by *faith*. The Law (Ten Commandments) is not based on *faith*. On the contrary, it says the person who does these things will live by them.

> Christ redeemed us from the curse of the Law, by becoming a curse for us, for it is written; cursed is everyone who is hung on a pole. He redeemed us, in order that the blessing given to Abraham might come to the gentiles through Christ Jesus, so that by *Faith* we might receive the promise of the spirit.

So in simplistic terms then, God's specific Grace for each of us is released by our Faith in Jesus Christ. It is a prerequisite of God that we get to Him through the Son, Jesus Christ, since the new dispensation was established by Christ for God at the cross. I mentioned "specific Grace," which is tailored by God for us *believers*. Also worthy of stating in comparison is that which is labeled as "general Grace." This is speaking to the standard blessings that all enjoy from God's creation—nature, the sun, moon, and the stars and all wildlife, the beaches, and all the natural beauties and elements that make up our known world. The benefit of the heat and light of the sun. The lesser of light, the moon, still emits light in smaller form in the evening. The appreciated beauty of the stars and the visible planets that we can observe. Trees for lumber, minerals are deposited all throughout the earth, including oil, natural gas, and geothermal heat. The tilted axis of the earth for the continuing of seasonal changes, and the distance that we are placed from the sun to advantage all the conditions that I have mentioned, and so, so much more that contribute to the concept that I am spotlighting here.

Now that is referring to the general Grace that is given by God for all mankind and the animals to enjoy and to benefit from. But in contrast, even in its majesty, revealing God's handiwork, it pales in comparison to the interdynamical workings of His New Covenant Law of the Grace and Truth and Peace of Jesus Christ that He releases to us *believers* in Jesus and the finished work on the Cross. It is extremely important that I develop this further here.

Yes, this is "meat and potatoes" information. This "specific Grace" is released to us when we "repent," which means to change our minds and understand that God is not mad at us, as the adversary would want us to believe as it is his effort to muddle, confuse, block, and stumble us from ever getting to these truths of our loving God, His plans for us, His almighty and radical love for us who hear His call and respond to it by allowing Him to love us as He wants to if we are only willing. "For Faith comes by hearing, by the hearing of the "Word" of Christ," as it says in Romans 10:17.

And that has been my experience, once the clear path to illumination was established in my spirit. If you need or want more *faith* (and who does not?) then get deeper in His *Word*. Expose yourself more to the mind, thoughts, and yes, the words of God as He has revealed to us through His Son who is the *Word* completely through our whole Bible. I can affirm that it is a proven and most worthy effort. Then His *Grace* and our *Faith* will do the rest.

The Mosaic Law was demand-conscious; it was performance-based, and emphasized man's effort to achieve a self-righteousness, which cannot be done. Well, plenty of effort maybe, just no self-righteousness. What was started in one garden (Eden) was finished in another (Gethsemane). We are fallen beings since the disobedience of Adam in the garden, sinful in nature and thus in the orchestration that God has employed to deliver us a construct within which we have free will, need for redemption, and a plan of salvation that we all have access to through His almighty being in which He possesses: omniscience, He knows perfectly all things; omnipresent, the ability to fill the whole universe in all its parts and be everywhere all at once; and omnipotence, the ability of God to do whatever He wills to do. Bearing these concepts out is very important to do to help us understand. One thing we can tend to do is try to anthropomorphize God—to attempt to limit or apply man's tendencies or limitations to God. That will not work nor help you to receive His Holy Spirit. For anyone to come to God, they must first believe that He "Is," just as it says in Hebrews 11:6, "And without *Faith* it is impossible to please God, because anyone who comes to him must *believe* that he exists and that he rewards those who earnestly seek him." God is a spirit, a nonphysical, nonmaterial being, who has always existed, without a beginning, and is pure love and all intelligence and completely righteousness simultaneously. It was out of His infinite love and intelligence that He had the desire for a family.

Jesus Christ is the firstborn of that divine intention. Resurrected, where He conquered death for us so that through His atonement for our sins and sinful nature we may have eternal life with the Father and our heavenly family in eternity for all that will accept, allow Him to carry us, and *believe* in Him as the propitiatory sacrifice for the sins of all mankind. He, Jesus Christ, was "the lamb of God" who takes away the sin of the world.

Yes, His royal and holy blood is way more than powerful enough to do just that, as the Holy Bible and all scriptures affirm. For just as we have a body, soul, and a spirit and as it says in Genesis 1:1, "We are made in the likeness of His image." We both are spiritual beings. And yes, we are made in His image. We possess a body (our temple), a mind, and a spirit, which is the life force from God within us. For His Holy Spirit is also a part of His Triune Godhead of Father, Son, and the Holy Spirit—one God with three functioning integral identities, one God, Jesus. By this same likeness, we have our being in Him also.

Remember, as we read before, "His yoke is easy, and His burden is light." Now, when your God tells you this and nothing has ever seemed to add up to that, then that is where the disconnect that I mentioned previously really became paramount, and it got me to dig into my study three years ago much deeper than I had before. Again, I will affirm that He, God, definitely is a rewarder of those that earnestly or diligently seek Him. As stated in Hebrews 11:6 and as mentioned just above, under the New Covenant and its dispensation established and released by Jesus Christ at the Cross, works and performance are no longer demanded of us redeemed *believers* for our salvation.

Yes, we will and should do works for God but not by demand any longer as this requirement was removed at the Cross. These things we do out of our love and Faith for and in Christ Jesus. Under Grace and Peace now, "when we rest, He works, and when He works, we rest." To fight our battles and enemies, we feed on His word and rest in Him, Christ Jesus, as we place all our worldly concerns, cares, and worries with Him at the foot of the Cross where our redemption was purchased and the power was released. Amen.

In Acts 15:5, there is a disagreement among the Jews and the Pharisees, with the apostles, once they had realized that the Apostle Paul was preaching the Gospel of Christ to the non-Jews (Gentiles), which had previously not been allowed. Then Peter had been given a similar message from the Holy Spirit, that all could be made clean by *believing* in Jesus Christ in the vision he had received in a dream from God.

In the dream, he had been directed by God that the old dispensation had been released; the rules of clean and unclean foods and also of clean and unclean people no longer applied. And here to his credit, he (Peter) steps up to confront and to stop the Jewish leaders from trying to derail the true Gospel message and reinsert their legalist and performance-based and now-defunct salvation plan as they attempt to put that back in place of the truth of the Gospel of the Grace and Truth of Jesus Christ.

We will pick it up here in Acts 15:5–21:

> Then some of the *believers* who belonged to the party of the Pharisees stood up and said, "The Gentiles must be circumcised and required to keep the Law of Moses." The apostles and the elders met to consider this question. After much discussion, Peter got up and addressed them: "Brothers, you know that some time ago God made a choice among you that the Gentiles might hear from my lips the message of the gospel and *believe*. God, who knows the heart, showed that He accepted them, by the giving of the Holy Spirit to them, for He purified their hearts by *faith*. Now then, why do you try to test them by putting on the necks of the Gentiles a yoke that we nor ancestors have been able to bear? No! We *believe* it is through the *Grace* of our Lord Jesus that we are saved, just as they are."

THERE IS A DOORWAY...

The whole assembly became silent as they listened to Barnabas and Paul telling, about the signs and wonders God had done among the Gentiles through them. When they had finished, James spoke up. "Brothers," he said, "listen to me. Simon has described to us how God first intervened to choose a people for His name from the Gentiles. The words of the prophets are-in-agreement with this, as it is written:

> "After this I will return
> And rebuild David's fallen tent.
> Its ruins I will rebuild,
> And I will restore it,
> that the rest of mankind may seek the Lord.
> Even all the Gentiles who bear my name.
> says the Lord, who does these things'—
> things known from long ago.

"It is my judgement, therefore, that we should not make it difficult for the Gentiles who are turning to God. Instead we should write to them, telling them to abstain from food polluted by idols, from sexual immorality, from the meat of strangled animals and from blood. For the Law of Moses has been preached in every city from the earliest times and is read in the synagogues on every Sabbath."

These scriptures here chronicle a major attempt to reintegrate the performance-based salvation plan of the Law here and has continued over the last two thousand years continually, where man and the churches have continually tried to tie our free gift of salvation to a performance-based one, whereby we are required to qualify for it or earn it in some manner that is used for control and submission to their authority as opposed to God's or Christ's. And this is *heresy*. In many instances, these very forces seek to pervert the word of God for many and various nefarious reasons.

Some are obviously out of ignorance, while many others are driven by much less excusable and unscrupulous behavior, namely, for a tethered congregational control and as well as the obvious collection plate or tithings of the constituents that they bind with their false doctrines. They know who they are and are guilty of following the errant way of Balaam, the using of the Gospel to attain personal wealth and riches. *Salvation of the people should be the primary motivation.*

They are in all actuality, whether they are aware of it or not, in league with the adversary, the evil one. In Matthew 10:8, Jesus commands the apostles, who are clear on this subject. It says in Matthew 10:8, "Heal the sick, raise the dead, cleanse those who have leprosy, drive out demons. Freely you have received; freely give." That in a nutshell is the preeminent effort of this work and composition on the *Word* of God to reveal the power and zeal that has been released with these undeniable truths, right out of His *Word*. It also says boldly in Ephesians 2:8–10:

> For it is by Grace you have been saved, through Faith—and this is not from yourselves, it is the Gift of God. Not by works, so that no one may boast. For we are God's handiwork, created in Christ Jesus to do good works, which God prepared in advance for us to do.

God's word, once clearly understood, is fully explanatory on this subject and all others that are integral to our grasping of the Gospel of the Grace, Peace, and the Truth of Jesus Christ. And it explains and warns of these threatening potentialities and attempts to attack, hobble, or stumble seekers from reaching or attaining this life-changing and mind-altering truths pertaining to our eternal salvation and, most importantly, the Godly wisdom and insight that gives us a relationship with our creator, our redemption, and acceptance into the eternal family of God.

Here is one of those most explicit warnings in Colossians 2:8–12:

> See to it that no one takes you captive through hollow and deceptive philosophy, which depends on human tradition and elemental spiritual forces of this world, rather than on Christ. For in Christ all the fullness of the deity lives in bodily form, And, in Christ you have been brought to fullness. He is the head over every power and authority.

This knowledge of truth and of scripture is the very foundation of the precepts that Martin Luther uncovered as a zealous Bible scholar when he challenged the church rulers on the misapplication of these doctrines, leading the Protestant movement away from the Catholic church and contributing directly to the Puritan movement, which caused the Pilgrims and others that were driven to leave Europe due to severe religious persecution.

This doctrinal strife resulted from the aforementioned nefarious motives that I cited before in this chapter, and these have continued to be a monumental stumbling block to God's people in the church over time, as they are not feeding the sheep as Christ has exampled but are meting out measured, partial doctrines, as well as inaccurate ones, or rather false doctrines and even heretical teachings as means to their ends.

Most of the time, the slippery slope starts with the wrong application of the meaning and applied inaccurate context in which they try to reinstitute the performance-demanding Law or the Ten Commandments to us *believers* today who are no longer under the law but under God's *Grace*, released at the Cross and established permanently for all time. For when He first revealed it to Father

Abraham, it was 420 years before the Law was given by Moses, a servant.

Now these former ordinances and commands of God are no longer required for our salvation as our Lord Jesus Christ has paid the cost for all mankind's redemption as our propitiatory and atoning sacrifice. God sent Christ Jesus to taste death so we do not have to. If we receive God's freely given gift of salvation and solely *believe* in the Son whom the Father sent, we achieve that, and not by any other way. Unfortunately, there have been several so-called versions of the gospel; there is only one true *Gospel*—the Law of His Grace by Faith. It is the one I am pulling directly from the scriptures and that I have chronicled all throughout this book, which I have backed up and verified.

Speaking of this Gospel, I will reference and cite here from Romans 1:16–17:

> For I am not ashamed of the Gospel, because it is the power of God that brings Salvation to everyone who believes: First to the Jew, then to the Gentile. For in the Gospel the righteousness of God is revealed—a righteousness that is by *faith* from first to last, just as it is written: "The righteous will live by *Faith*."

And a mighty amen to that! Continuing now to address this meat-and-potatoes knowledge of our true Gospel of the Grace and Truth of Jesus Christ, we will stay in Romans and further examine and support these truths with the Apostle Paul's Holy Spirit–revealed teachings in Romans 10:1–13, for it also is pivotal. Romans 10:1–15 says:

> Brothers and sisters, my heart's desire in prayer to God for the Israelites is that they may be saved. I can testify about them that they are zealous for God, but their zeal is not based on knowledge. Since they did not know the righ-

teousness of God and sought to establish their own, they did not submit to God's righteousness. Christ is the culmination of the Law so that there may be righteousness for everyone who *believes*. Moses writes this about the righteousness that is by the Law: "The person who does these things will live by them." But the righteousness that is by *faith* says: do not say in your heart who will ascend into heaven? (that is to bring Christ down) or, who will descend into the deep? (that is to bring Christ up from the dead). But what does it say? The word is near you; It is in your mouth and in your heart, that is, the message concerning *faith* that we proclaim: If you declare with your mouth, "Jesus is Lord", and *believe* in your heart that God raised him from the dead, you will be saved. For it is with your heart that you *believe and are justified,* and it is with your mouth that you profess your Faith and are saved. As Scripture says, "Anyone who *believes* in Him will never be put to shame. For there is no difference between Jew and Gentile—the same Lord is Lord of all and richly blesses all who call on Him, for, "Everyone who calls on the name of the Lord will be saved." How, then, can they call on the one whom they have not *believed in*? And how can they *believe* in the one whom they have not heard? And how can they hear without someone preaching to them? And how can anyone preach unless they are sent? As it is written: "How beautiful, is the feet of those who bring the good news!"

I must not stop here but continue with the next critical verses. Still reading in Romans 10 and continuing with verse 16:

> But not all the Israelites accepted the good news. For Isaiah says, Lord, who has believed our message? Consequently, Faith comes from hearing the message, and the message is heard through the word about Christ. But I ask, did they not hear? Of course, they did.

This is my calling and mission, as stated here in Luke 10:2 and why this is no light matter to me. Luke 10:2–3 says:

> He was saying to them, "The harvest is abundant (for there are many who need to hear the good news about salvation), but the workers are few. Therefore, (prayerfully) ask the Lord of the harvest to send out workers into His harvest. Go your own way; listen carefully: I am sending you out like lambs among wolves."

I suggest it is no different today, and in my spirit, I have received and heard the calling of our Lord and Savior, God the Father, Son, and Holy Spirit; all three are of one accord and are God, and He has shown me this unequivocally to where my purpose forward is no longer a mystery, as all things were prior to these life-changing and extremely powerful revelations and the knowledge that the Spirit of Truth has revealed through His Word.

In the following paragraphs, I will be highlighting and reviewing scriptures in an effort to develop and firm up the meaning and understanding behind this concept more fully on God's *Grace*. I will be stacking them in a machine-like, rapid-fire succession for the saturation and deeper understanding of this most powerful dynamic of God's power and love. Acts 13:38–47 says:

> Therefore my friends, I want you to know that through Jesus the forgiveness of sins is proclaimed to you. Through him, everyone who *believes* is set free from every sin, a justification

you were not able to obtain under the Law of Moses. Take care that what the prophets have said does not happen to you: "Look you scoffers, wonder and perish, for I am going to do something in your days that you would never believe even if someone told you. As Paul and Barnabas were leaving the synagogue, the people invited them to speak further about these things on the next Sabbath. When the congregation was dismissed, many of the Jews and devout converts to Judaism followed Paul and Barnabas, who talked with them and urged them to continue in the *Grace* of God. On the next Sabbath, almost the whole city gathered to hear the word of the Lord. When the Jews saw the crowds, they were filled with jealousy. They began to contradict what Paul was saying and heaped abuse upon him. Then Paul and Barnabas answered them boldly: "We had to speak the word of God to you first. Since you reject it and do not consider yourselves worthy of eternal life, we now turn to the Gentiles. "For this is what the Lord has commanded us:

> "I have made you a light for the
> Gentiles.
> That you may bring salvation to the
> Ends of the earth."

Quite a bit of information covering a wide swath in that last scripture group there. Read it again, even two or three times. Read it out loud also if there is an opportunity, for there is much power in the speaking and the hearing of Holy Scripture. In the next verse cited, Paul is testifying before King Agrippa on his conversion on the road to Damascus where the Lord appeared and converted him with His presence, immediately blinding Paul and burning him intensely.

Here are the words of his conversion on trial before the king in Acts 26:12–18:

> On one of these journeys I was going to Damascus with the authority and Commission of the chief priests. About noon, King Agrippa, as I was on the road, I saw a light from heaven, brighter than the sun, blazing around me and my companions. We all fell to the ground, and I heard a voice saying to me in Aramaic, "Saul, Saul, why do you persecute me?" "It is hard for you to kick against the goads." Then I asked, "who are you Lord?" "I am Jesus whom you are persecuting, the Lord replied." "Now get up and stand on your feet. I have appeared to you to appoint you as a servant and as a witness of what you have seen and will see of me. I will rescue you from your own people and from the gentiles. I am sending you to them, to open their eyes and turn them from darkness to light, and from the power of Satan to God, so that they may receive forgiveness of sins and a place among those who are sanctified by *Faith* in me."

The resurrected Christ appearing directly in front of you in His glorified presence may be a lot or too much intensity of divine power and righteousness to be in anyone's presence without our eternal inherited bodies. Poor Saul, soon to be called Paul.

Also, in the chapter of Acts 20:32, it says, "Now I commit you to God and to the Word of his *Grace*, which can build you up and give you an inheritance among all those who are sanctified." In Acts 4:33–35, we get another glimpse of the broadness of this power of God's *Grace*.

> With great power the apostles continued to testify to the resurrection of the Lord Jesus. And God's *Grace* was so powerfully at work in

> them all that there were no needy persons among them. For from time to time, those who owned land or houses sold them, brought the money from the sales, and put it at the apostle's feet, and it was distributed to anyone who had need.

That is some good insight and evidence of the potential and capability and power of God's love and provision for us—His Grace! Continuing in Acts 14:2–7:

> But the Jews who refused to believe in Jesus as Messiah, stirred up the other gentiles and poisoned their minds against the brothers. So Paul and Barnabas spent considerable time there, speaking boldly for the Lord, who confirmed the message of his Grace by enabling them to perform signs and wonders. the people of the city were divided; Some sided with the Jews, others with the apostles. there was a plot afoot among both gentiles and Jews, together with their leaders, to mistreat them and stone them. but they found out about it and fled to the Lycaonia and cities of Lystra and Derbe', and to the surrounding country, where they continued to preach the Gospel.

I am now going to move into one of my favorite books of the Bible, the Thessalonians, both books. It is for the informational truths it contains, like all of Paul's writings or the "Pauline" writings, and the most revelatory concepts they lay out. Beginning in 1 Thessalonians 1:2–3:

> We give thanks always for all of you, continually mentioning you in our prayers; recalling unceasingly before our God and Father your work energized by Faith, and your service moti-

vated by love and unwavering hope in (the return of) our Lord Jesus Christ.

Again in 1 Thessalonians 4:3, it expounds on our sanctification, our being claimed by God, redeemed, and set aside for His will and purposes now and in eternity to come. In 1 Thessalonians 4:3–12, it says:

> It is Gods will that you be sanctified: that you should avoid sexual immorality; that each of you should learn to control your own body in a way that is holy and honorable, not in passionate lusts like the pagans, who do not know God; and in this manner no one should wrong or take advantage of a brother or sister. The Lord will punish all those who commit such sins, as we told you and warned you before. For God did not call us to be impure, but to live a holy life. Therefore, anyone who rejects this instruction does not reject a human being but God, the very God who gives you His Holy Spirit. Now about your love for one another we do not need to write to you, for you yourselves have been taught by God to love each other. And in fact, you do love all God's family throughout Macedonia. Yet we urge you, brothers and sisters, to do so more and more. and to make it your ambition to lead a quiet life; You should mind your own business and work with your hands, just as we told you, so that your daily life may win the respect of the outsiders and so you will not be dependent on anybody."

As I stated before, these small chapters in the writings of Paul contain powerful information in them. Another scripture from 1 Thessalonians 4:14–18:

> For if we *believe* that Jesus died and rose again, and so we *believe* that God will bring with Jesus those that have fallen asleep in him. According to the Lord's word, we tell you that we who are still alive, who are left until the coming of the Lord, will certainly not precede those that have fallen asleep. For the Lord Himself will come down from heaven, with a loud command, with the voice of the archangel and the trumpet call of God, and the dead in Christ will rise first. After that, we who are still alive and left will be caught up into the clouds to meet the Lord in the air. And so, we will be with the Lord forever. Therefore encourage one another with these words.

And here, some final instructions from Paul in 1 Thessalonians 5:14–24; it says just what the Holy Spirit revealed:

> And we urge you, brothers and sisters, warn those who are idle and disruptive, encourage the disheartened, help the weak, be patient with everyone. Make sure that nobody pays back wrong for wrong, but always strive to do what is good for each other and for everyone else. Rejoice always, pray continually, give thanks in all circumstances; for this is God's will for you in Jesus Christ.
>
> Do not quench the spirit. Do not treat prophecies with contempt but test them all; hold on to what is good, reject every kind of evil. May God himself, the God of peace, sanctify you through and through. May your whole spirit, soul and body be kept blameless at the coming of our Lord Jesus Christ. The one who calls you is *faithful*, and he will do it.

We're leaving 1 Thessalonians and moving into its (Grace's) usage and looking at the two places where it is referenced and moving into the second book of Thessalonians now in the two places that the word *Grace* is employed directly, 2 Thessalonians 1:4–12:

> Therefore, among Gods churches we boast about your perseverance and *faith* in all the persecutions and trials you are enduring. All this is evidence that God's judgement is right, and as a result you will be counted worthy of the kingdom of God, for which you are suffering. God is just: He will pay back trouble to those that trouble you and give relief to you that are troubled, and to us all as well. This will happen when the Lord Jesus is revealed from heaven in a blazing fire with his powerful Angels. He will punish those who do not know God and do not obey the Gospel of our Lord Jesus. They will be punished with everlasting destruction and shut out from the presence of the Lord and from the glory of his might on the day he comes to be glorified in his holy people and to be marveled at among all those who have *believed*. This includes you because you *believed* our testimony to you.
>
> With this in mind, we constantly pray for you, that our God may make you worthy of his calling, and that by his power he may bring to fruition your every desire for goodness and your every deed prompted by *Faith*. We pray this so that the name of our Lord Jesus may be glorified in you, and you in him, according to the *Grace* of our God and the Lord Jesus Christ.

These verses reveal the richness, love, and compassion our God, Lord, and Savior has for us, His *faithful* children. This is the *Grace* of God, His overflowing provision, plan for our redemption, and the coming eternal paradisial existence with God. Oh, how great our mighty God is. He is our El Shaddai (Almighty God), and we are completely His handiwork; He is the conductor and orchestrator of this grand symphony of our reality in the wiles of this "seemingly" random existence. But it so not.

This craftily conceived divination of our reality by God almighty, the very actuality that out of all the other possibilities, is divine, providential, guided, and ordered by the great, majestic, nonmaterial spirit, God, that created everything we see and know of in this universe and galaxy, out of nothing, ex-nihilo. In His omnipotence, omniscience, and omnipresence, God has created a reality where we have our existence, are given a free will to exercise, and choose, if we will, to recognize the sovereign being responsible. The *one* true God that has established a just and righteous program of redeeming all the lost, or fallen souls, from an irresponsible act and giving us the free will that He in His forbearance and wisdom established a righteous platform to do so, even if doing so by Himself.

One more scripture to add here from 2 Thessalonians further explains *Grace*, with Paul encouraging the Thessalonians to stand firm in 2:13–17:

> But we ought always to thank God for you, brothers and sisters loved by the Lord, because God chose you as first-fruits to be saved through the sanctifying work of the Spirit and through *belief* in the truth (*Faith*). He called you to this through our Gospel, that you might share in the Glory of our Lord Jesus Christ. So then, brothers and sisters, stand firm and hold fast to the teachings we passed on to you, whether by word of mouth or by letter. May our Lord Jesus Christ himself and God our Father, who loved us and by his *Grace* gave us eternal encouragement and good hope, encourage your hearts and strengthen you in every good deed and word.

Amen.

First, we must feed on milk and honey. Then we will move to more of a meat and potatoes meal. When ready and well-nourished, thirdly, we move to the bread and the wine. Eventually, we wind up with the bread of life and the living water, the fountain of life. We do not stand on our righteousness; we rest in His. We are not blessed according to us but by His saving *Grace* and His righteousness as we look away from ourselves and look always to Jesus Christ. As He is, so are we in this world.

Yes, we rest in Jesus, Yeshua, which means salvation. *Grace* can only work for sinners. Their need attracts God's power. We must recognize the need we have for the savior so He can fill it. Until we recognize our need for His power, His specific *Grace* for us is held back and is released according to His will when we do. When the spirit of God is with us, it softens our spirit and keeps us receptive and operating in a mode of love.

If you are giving it, you are in the right mode to receive it. God's love is His *Grace*. Hebrews 10:29 calls the Holy Spirit the "Spirit of Grace." It is God's will that you be sanctified. Avoid sexual immorality. Do good, and silence the ignorant talk of foolish people. Suffer for good rather than do evil. Give thanks in all things. Love Jesus/God, and seek him diligently. Have life in Him more abundantly. Persevere in all trials. Walk in the Spirit of and have *Faith* in God/Jesus/Yeshua. God does not force, He offers.

We must accept/*believe* to allow His blessings to flow. Our *Faith* is the currency that powers God's engine of *Grace* and love, of abundance and provision. It is not your obedience, although it does matter; you enter the kingdom of God by *Faith* in Jesus Christ and the finished work of the cross alone. And that, my friends, is true *Grace*. Undeserved, unmerited, unearned favor. Winding down this chapter on our being *saved by Grace through Faith*, we will look at the apostle John's later epistles just before Jude and Revelation. In 1 John 1:5–10 and 2:1–2, it says:

> This is the message we have heard from him
> and declare to you: God is light; in Him there is

> no darkness at all. If we claim to have fellowship with him and yet we walk in the darkness, we lie and do not live out the truth. But if we walk in the light, as he is in the light, we have fellowship with one another, and the blood of Jesus, His Son purifies us from all sin. If we claim to be without sin, we deceive ourselves and the truth is not in us. If we confess our sins, he is *faithful* and just and will forgive our sins and purify us from all unrighteousness. If we claimed we have not sinned, we make Him out to be a liar and His word is not in us.
>
> My dear children, I write this to you so that you will not sin. But if anybody does sin, we have an advocate with the Father—Jesus Christ, the Righteous One. He is the atoning sacrifice for our sins, and not only ours but for all the sins of the whole world.

The verse 1 John 3:16 is as powerful as John 3:16, one of the most pivotal and recognized scripture in the New Covenant. It says in 1 John 3:16–24:

> This is how we know what love is: Jesus Christ laid down his life for us. And we ought to lay our lives for our brothers and sisters. If anyone has material possessions and sees a brother or sister in need but has no pity on them, how can the love of God be in that person? Dear children, let us not love with words or speech but with actions and in truth. This is how we know that we belong to the truth and how we set our hearts at rest in his presence: If our hearts condemn us, we know that God is greater than our hearts, and he knows everything. Dear friends, if our hearts do

not condemn us, we have confidence before God and receive from him anything we ask, because we keep his commands and do what pleases him. And this is his command: to *believe* in the name of His Son, Jesus Christ, and to love one another as he commanded us. The one who keeps God's commands lives in him, and he in them. And this is how we know that he lives in us, we know it by the spirit he gave us.

And again, inspiring information of knowledge and truth is given further in 1 John 4:2–21:

> This is how you can recognize the spirit of God: every spirit that acknowledges that Jesus Christ has come in the flesh is from God. But every spirit that does not acknowledge Jesus is not from God. This is the spirit of the Antichrist, which you have heard is coming and now is already in the world. For you, dear children, are from God and have overcome them, because the one who is in you is greater than the one who is in the world. They are from the world and therefore speak from the viewpoint of the world, and the world listens to them. We are from God, and whoever is not from God does not listen to us. This is how we recognize the spirit of truth and the spirit of falsehood. Dear friends let us love one another, for love comes from God. Everyone who loves has been born of God and knows God. Whoever does not love does not know God, because *God is love*. This is how God showed his love among us: he sent his one and only son into the world that we might live through him. This is love: not that we loved God, but that he loved us and sent his son as an atoning sacrifice for our

> sins. Dear friends, since God so loved us, we also ought to love one another. No one has ever seen God, but if we love one another, God lives in us and his love is made complete in us. This is how we know that we live in him and he in us: he has given us of his spirit. And we have seen and testify that the father has sent his son to be the savior of the world. If anyone acknowledges that Jesus is the son of God, God lives in them and they in God. And so we know and rely on the love God has for us. *God is love.* Whoever lives in love lives in God, and God in them. This is how love is made complete among us so that we will have confidence on the day of judgment: in this world we are like Jesus. There is No Fear in love. But perfect love drives out fear, because fear has to do with punishment. The one who fears is not made perfect in love. We love because he first loved us. Whoever claims to love God yet hates a brother or sister is a liar. For whoever does not love their brother and sister, whom they have seen cannot love God, whom they have not seen. And he has given us this command: anyone who loves God must also love their brother and sister.

That is a mighty, powerful scripture loaded with wisdom and much truthful information. Read it many times. Aloud even. Following still in 1 John, with continued dynamic information in the scriptures, we continue in chapter 5:1–12:

> Everyone who *believes* that Jesus is the Christ is born of God, and everyone who loves the father, loves his child as well. This is how we know that we love the children of God: by loving God and carrying out his commands. In fact, this is love for God: to keep his commands. And

his commands are not burdensome, for everyone born of God overcomes the world. This is the victory that has overcome the world, even our *Faith*. Who is it that overcomes the world? Only the one who *believes* that Jesus is the son of God. This is the one who came by water and blood, Jesus Christ. He did not come by water only, but by water and blood. And it is the Holy Spirit who testifies, because the Holy Spirit is the Truth. For there are three that testify; the spirit, the water and the blood; And the three are in agreement. We accept human testimony, but God's testimony is greater because it is the testimony of God, which he has given about his son. Whoever *believes* in the son of God accepts this testimony period whoever does not *believe* God has made him out to be a liar because they have not *believed* the testimony God has given about his son. And this is the testimony: God has given us eternal life and this life is in his son. Whoever has the son has life; Whoever does not have the son of God does not have life.

Progressing on now to 2 John 1:1–11:

The elder, to the lady chosen by God and to her children, whom I love in the truth—and not I only, but also all who know the truth because of the truth, which lives in us and will be with us forever: "*Grace*, mercy and peace", from God the Father and from Jesus Christ, the father's son, will be with us in truth and love. It has given me great joy to find some of your children walking in the truth, just as the father commanded us. And now, dear lady I am not writing you a new command but one we have had from the beginning.

THERE IS A DOORWAY...

> I ask that we love one another. And this is love: That we walk in obedience to his commands. As you have heard from the beginning, his command is that you walk in love. I say this because many deceivers, who do not acknowledge Jesus Christ as coming in the flesh gone out into the world. Any such person is it is the deceiver and the Antichrist. Watch out that you do not lose what we have worked for, but that you may be rewarded fully. Anyone who runs ahead and does not continue in the teaching of Christ does not have God: whoever continues in the teaching, has both the Father and the Son. If anyone comes to you and does not bring this teaching, do not take them into your house or welcome them. Anyone who welcomes them shares in their wicked work.

These revelations, if landing and compiling in your understanding and knowledge, should be building and supporting a foundational base to yield you to a more complete awareness of God's purpose, power, direct control, and ultimate authority over us and all things. As he says in His Word, "All things work together for the good purposes of those that love God." I have stated several places in this book that Jesus is God's *Grace* given to and for us—our sanctification, justification, and redemption back to the Father by the Son. This verse in Titus states this rather clearly in support of this assertion, and I will close this most momentous chapter of this book with it. Titus 2:11–15 and finish in 3:1–7 where it continues:

> For the *Grace* of God has appeared that offers Salvation to all people. It teaches us to say no to ungodliness and worldly passions, and to live self-controlled, upright and godly lives in this present age, while we wait for the blessed hope the appearing of the glory of our great God and savior, Jesus Christ, who gave himself for us

to redeem us from all wickedness and to purify for himself a people that are his very own, eager to do what is good. these, then, are the things you should teach. Encourage and rebuke with all authority. Do not let anyone despise you.

Now Titus 3:1–7 says:

"Remind the people to be subject to rulers and authorities, to be obedient, to be ready to do whatever is good, to slander no one, to be peaceable and considerate and always to be gentle toward everyone. At one time we were foolish, disobedient, deceived and enslaved by all kinds of passions and pleasures. We lived in malice and envy, being hated and hating one another. But when the kindness and love of God our savior appeared, He saved us, not because of righteous things we had done, but because of His *Grace*. He saved us through the washing of rebirth and renewal by the Holy Spirit., Whom He poured out on us generously through Jesus Christ our savior, so that, having been justified by His *Grace*, we might become heirs, having the hope of eternal life.

Amen. To Almighty God, El Shaddai, be the *glory*, the *majesty*, and the *power* forever.

Chapter 5

The Doorway

As a boy of ten and a half or eleven, and upon being recently led to Christ, my awareness and ideas of Jesus, God, and what religion was began to be broadened. At that time, I had been given my first Bible, a small red New Testament of the Holy Scriptures, which I began to read to discover what was beheld in the words of scripture and the doctrine that had been introduced to me through my extended family and the churches I attended with my family as a little guy.

Christmas and Easter were a time where we all dressed up for church as we went on the holidays and Sundays as a family while we were still together. At that time, my walk to an understanding of the word of God was beginning to take shape. As I began to read in Matthew, the first book of the New Testament, I knew that what I was reading was most profound. It seemed as if in no time, somehow, I knew this wisdom and knowledge surrounding Jesus was likely supranatural, and outside knowledge was being transferred someway, somehow from a most divine and invested being.

The fact that I was able to comprehend so complex a concept at such a young age or was even concerned enough to contemplate such ideas that I can now assuredly say that it was a leading and early drawing of my spirit by God's Spirit. I somehow was imbued with some outside, imported understanding that the wisdom and knowledge that I was having revealed to me was not of this world. Of that, at eleven or twelve years old, I was certain.

There was a nugget of wisdom or promise in His word to us that hooked me very early on, and that I, without a critically accurate understanding, bit into and bought and believed God in His words to us through the disciples. Namely, in my early reading in Matthew, I uncovered a gem that had begun and led my quest all the way to this day, almost fifty years down the trail. That little nugget of wisdom and promise was of more value than fine gold.

I still remember that time from my youthful inquiring of His word, as if it were yesterday. Matthew 7:7–8 set the fishhook in my jowls for life.

> Ask and it will be given to you; Seek and you will find; Knock and the *door* will be opened to you. For everyone who asks receives; the one who seeks finds; and to the one who knocks, the *door* will be opened.

Now I am going to go out on a limb here and say that obviously everyone that reads these words may not have that same effect, response, or understanding, for I believe that is in the hands and the mind of God—that is, Jesus Christ, who is the Aleph and the Taph, the Alpha and the Omega, the beginning and the end of all things. For in Colossians 1:15–20, it says, and this is extremely powerful:

> The Son is the image of the invisible God, the first-born over all creation. For in him all things were created: things in heaven and on earth, visible and invisible, whether thrones or powers or rulers or authorities; All these things have been created through him and for him. He is before all things, and in Him all things hold together. And he is the head of the body, the church; He is the beginning and the first born from among the dead, so that in everything he might have the supremacy. For God was pleased to have all his fullness dwell in him, and through

him to reconcile to himself all things, whether things on earth or things in heaven, by making peace through his blood, shed on the Cross.

That's right, and it is just as it says and as you read—He is the very force that began the *big bang*, and more directly, He is the mysterious force that science cannot explain that holds people on this planet spinning at over one thousand miles per hour—that is, even gravity, itself. The revelation and the mysteries of God were hidden in the times of old but have been so revealed to us in His word, the Holy Scriptures, and through God's only begotten Son Jesus Christ, the prophesied Messiah of the Hebrew people. It was predicted over 1,500 years before the fullness of time for Him to intervene in human affairs and redeem the children of God by the Old Testament prophets when He would come to earth, the time of His physical visitation.

In Matthew 7:13, the verses begin and are captioned "The Narrow and Wide Gates." In Luke 13:23, these verses are captioned "The Narrow Door," referring to the same parable taught to them by Jesus. We will look at both and compare. Matthew 7:13 says:

> Enter through the narrow gate. For wide is the gate and broad is the road that leads to destruction, and many enter through it. But small is the gate and narrow the road that leads to life, and only a few find it.

In Luke 13:23–30, it says:

> Someone asked him, "Lord are only a few people going to be saved?" He said to them, "Make every effort to enter through the narrow *door*, because many I tell you will try to enter and will not be able to. Once the owner of the house gets up and closes the *door*, you will stand outside,—knocking and pleading, "Sir, open the *door* for us." "But he will answer you, I don't know

> you or where you come from." "Then you will say, 'We ate and drank with you, and you taught in our streets.'" But he will reply, 'I don't know you or where you come from. Away from me, all you evil doers!' "There will be weeping there, and gnashing of teeth, when you see Abraham, Isaac and Jacob and all the prophets in the kingdom of God, but you yourselves thrown out. People will come from east and west and north and south and will take their places at the feast in the kingdom of God. Indeed, there are those who are last who will be first, and first who will be last.

The two concepts that immediately jumped out to me from these two interpretations of the same parable are the two concepts listed, which referred to the road to destruction and the road that leads to life—two choices that immediately bring to mind the poster that many of us have seen. That is probably taken from a poem written that speaks of the road less traveled by. It has been my experience that many of the lessons that we learn along the road of life, through the school of hard knocks, so to speak, where there are morality lessons learned experientially, and they mirror or affirm many of the concepts of Bible theology.

Scripturally referring to a choice of path for us to take by the advice of the creator of the universe and the very concept of a life choice of direction is exactly what Robert Frost is referencing in this wise and quaint poem. This is simply a reflection of the most miraculous concept of ours from scripture, which affirms, "The Lord works in mysterious ways." At this time, I would like to bring in a few scriptures to support the statement that was just made above and its assertion.

In Deuteronomy 32:4, it says:

> He is the rock, his works are perfect, and all his ways are just. A *faithful* God who does no wrong, upright and just is he.

THERE IS A DOORWAY...

Also in Ecclesiastes 11:5, it says:

> As you do not know the path of the wind, or how the body is formed in a mother's womb, so you cannot understand the work of God, the maker of all things.

Thus spanning all the way from the early books of Moses through to the last book of the New Testament in Revelation, where it says in Revelation 15:2–4:

> They held harps given to them by God. And sang the song of God's servant Moses and of the Lamb: "Great and marvelous are your deeds, Lord God Almighty. Just and true are your ways, King of nations. For whom will not fear you Lord and bring glory to your name? For you alone are Holy. All nations will come in worship before you for your righteous acts have been revealed."

Another verse in Matthew adds to the compilation of scripture I am using to help flesh out the concept in many facets to the reference of "the *doorway*." It is captioned above the verses, "Seven Woes on the Teachers of the Law and the Pharisees" in Matthew 23:13–24:

> Woe to you, teachers of the Law and Pharisees, you hypocrites! You shut the *door* of the kingdom of heaven in people's faces. You yourselves do not enter, nor will you let those enter who are trying to. Woe to you, teachers of the Law and Pharisees, you hypocrites! You travel overland and seek to win a single convert, and when you have succeeded, you make them twice as much a child of hell as you are. Woe to you, blind guides! You say, if anyone swears by the temple, it means nothing; but anyone who

swears by the gold of the temple is bound by that oath. You blind fool's, which is greater: the gold, or the temple that makes the gold sacred? You also say, if anyone swears by the altar, it means nothing: but anyone who swears by the gift on the altar is bound by that oath. You blind men! Which is greater: the gift, or the altar that makes the gift sacred? Therefore anyone who swears by the altar swears by it and everything on it. And anyone who swears by the temple swears by it and by the one who dwells in it. And anyone who swears by heaven swears by God's throne, and by the one who sits on it. Woe to you, teachers of the Law and Pharisees, you hypocrites! You give a 10th of your spices—mint, dill and cumin. But you have neglected the more important matters of the Law—Justice, mercy and *faithfulness*. You strain out a gnat, but, swallow a camel.

There is a good bit of meat to flesh out here from the above just mentioned scripture (Pun intended!) beginning in Matthew 23:13; this is a strongly worded and very powerful condemnation of the Hebrews by Jesus as He spoke to the crowds. It is here He calls their teachers hypocrites and boldly accuses them of blocking those they are teaching from entering through the *door* to the kingdom of heaven, which is part of the reasoning for the purpose of this book—to attract, clarify, and hopefully enlighten the readers to explore further the Holy Scriptures and to glorify the Father, the Son, and the Holy Spirit and reveal the true Gospel of the Grace, Peace, and Truth of Jesus Christ and uncover some of the layers of false doctrine and teachings that have plagued the church of God's people by wrong interpretation or even purposeful misdirection.

A large piece to what was a most mysterious puzzle for the longest of time that stumbled and eluded me of a clearer understanding of scripture came in the form of a few short but incredibly impactful scriptures that provided the understanding and clarity that busted down barriers and revealed the truth as it had not been taught to me before. To the point of saturation and the level of grasping that I now am in possession of, here they follow. Matthew 6:33 says, "But seek first his kingdom and his righteousness, and all these things will be given to you as well."

Therein lay the problem, for in my limited understanding, I was not clear on what exactly God's kingdom was, other than my assumption that it spoke of the heavenly kingdom. Then by following the scriptural teaching of Pastor Joseph Prince's sermons and by reading his book *Live the Let Go Life*, on pages 45–47, all the words and concepts aligned in one moment as I was introduced to the true teachings of Christ and the accurate Gospel of Grace that had now been revealed to me.

On page 46, as I read those words of Romans 14:17, the pieces, as I digested this one scripture, began to fall into place. And here it is:

> For the kingdom of God is not a matter of eating and drinking, but of righteousness, peace and joy in the Holy Spirit. Because anyone who serves Christ. In this way it is pleasing to God and receives human approval.

And now, with my fuller understanding expanding and growing in the knowledge of His *Grace*, coupled with this revelation of truth about what the kingdom is and how it is wrapped up in our seeking Christ's salvation and His righteousness and not our own. I was on my enlightened way. How that scripture had never been taught or had not been revealed to me or had I ever even any exposure to it, I am not sure.

Now I have latched onto something meaty, but not quite fully yet. This "righteousness" thing still had me a little confused, for the only understanding I had previously was the thought that I must earn or establish my righteousness by my performance or behavior by the misinterpretation of the application of the Ten Commandments. And that, over my lifetime, one day, I may arrive at or achieve that. That wrongful teaching has been horribly mistaught, misconstrued, and wrongly permeates a great deal of the churches of today.

So the pertinent information needed to clarify this wrong teaching that is eerily pervasive in the houses of worship of attempting believers and followers of the word of God was this next most important, in my opinion, scripture. In 2 Corinthians 5:21, it says, "God made him who had no sin, to be sin for us, so that in him we might become the righteousness of God." Along with these scriptures, there are a few more that help to drive the concept home. Ephesians 2:8 adds, "For it is by Grace you have been saved, through Faith—and this is not from yourselves, it is the gift of God." So by believing in the Messiah, the Christ Jesus our Lord and Savior, and that alone and not by works, as this next verse affirms.

In Romans 3:21–26, the caption that is above these verses is titled "Righteousness by Faith,"

> "But now apart from the Law. The righteousness of God has been made known, to which the Law and the prophets testify. This righteousness is given through *Faith* in Jesus Christ to all who *believe* in and on him." There is no difference between Jew and Gentile, For all have sinned and fall short of the glory of God. And all are justified freely by his *Grace* through the redemption that came by Christ Jesus. God presented Christ as a sacrifice of atonement, through the shedding of his blood—to be received by *Faith*. He did this to demonstrate his righteousness, because in his forbearance he had left the sins committed beforehand unpunished—He did it to demonstrate his righteousness at the present time, so-as-to be just and the one who justifies those who have *Faith* in Jesus.

Now clearly these last few scriptures did not have in them the words *door* or *doorway*. However, they directly infer and steer us to that *door*. The *doorway* is further affirmed in Paul's letter in 2 Timothy 1:9, "He has saved us and called us to a holy life—not because of anything we have done but because of his own purpose and *Grace*." This *Grace* was given to us in Christ Jesus since the beginning of time. In Galatians 3:14, it is further asserted and affirmed, "He redeemed us in order that the blessing given to Abraham might come to the Gentiles through Christ Jesus, so that by *Faith* we might receive the promise of the spirit." Jesus is *Grace*. He is the *doorway* and the *good shepherd*. It truly was this very nugget of golden knowledge that in its preponderance and of which will be developed much further in the chapter "We Are Saved by Grace through Faith."

One of the recurring themes or motivating factors of this book is the fact that from the time that I began to read God's Word at the age of ten or eleven, with limited understanding, and almost ashamedly so, that it took to the age of fifty-eight years old for me to get a more concrete understanding. But God's timing is perfect. Now, I have competently come to understand God's plan for mankind and have gained by revelation from reading His Word and through persistent study, continuing to wash daily in His Word as the Holy Spirit has guided me over the last several years.

As I have washed daily in His Word, bathed in it even to a level of saturation, where, praise God, it finally broke through to a point where I can say, I have been illuminated by the light of the Holy Spirit of God's Word. Yes, the all-elusive enlightenment of this reality. No, one can know it all, and it will be a lifelong, continued discovery and evolution of my *Faith* and my understanding. For even though I feel I have been given illumination, there is still far much more for me to learn. That is what I am trying to share here with you.

Prayerfully, I am most hopeful that if nothing else, if these pearls of wisdom do not deliver powerful and direct knowledge of God, that I pray, at least, that it takes you to His written word to find out for yourself, and hopefully, even more than you already have. Amen.

Now onward through the *doorway*. We know that the whole of the Bible is the inspired word of God. It is inspired by God, given to man to write down, as He told them to do, wherever, that He did not write it Himself. As I have stated previously, it is literally from the front cover to the back. The complete story of God, of Jesus Christ, in print in the Old Testament and New alike (or Covenant) as I have suggested. And once we dispense with the less accurate terminology of Testament and replace it with Covenant, the picture gets a little clearer.

Even so, it is completely God's word revealed to man, and that I take the wisdom, the story of God's chosen people, Israel's history, and the knowledge of Him from the Old Covenant and the New alike. And moving now back to our *door* themed scripture verses and the scripture I will quote here is from the book of Proverbs, which is written by Solomon, the wisest man to have ever lived, short of Jesus Christ himself, who was a God-man. The result of the mixture of God's Holy Spirit with the Virgin Mary, birthing the Christ Jesus and delivering to us our eventual, eternal savior, redeemer, and God. Proverbs 8:34–36 says:

> Blessed are those who listen to me, watching daily at my *doors*, waiting at my *doorway*. For those who find me find life and receive favor from the LORD. But those who fail to find me harm themselves; all who hate me love death.

Now it is here that some of these years of study come to my benefit. For upon close inspection of the Old Testament, which we have established would be more accurately rendered Old Covenant, is contained the old Mosaic Law, which was fulfilled and supplanted or replaced by Jesus Christ's message and Law of Grace and Peace and Truth and the finished work at the Cross, thereby replacing the old Law given by Moses. For the word says in the Gospel of John in 1:17, "Moses gave the Law, but Grace and Truth came by Jesus Christ."

Whenever you come to the word *LORD* in the Bible, if it is in all uppercase, then it is speaking of Jehovah God, the I am that I am, from the burning bush where Jehovah God spoke to Moses and gave him the Law. And conversely, when you come to the word *Lord with* capital *L* and lowercase *ord*, it is speaking of God the son Jesus Christ. In these Old Testament Psalms and Proverbs, God is revealing His nature and the nature of His coming son at the same time.

THERE IS A DOORWAY...

In these revelations that He inspires to David and Solomon, they reveal revelations and great insights into the heart of God and His divine power in these powerfully inspired scriptures. Following is the scripture out of Exodus 12:21–30:

> Then Moses summoned all of the Elders of Israel and said to them, go at once and select the animals for your families and slaughter the Passover lamb. Take a bunch of hyssop, dip it into the blood in the basin and put some of the blood on the top and on both sides of the *door* frame. None of you shall go out of the *door* of your house until morning. When the Lord goes through the land to strike down the Egyptians, He will see the blood on top of and sides of the *door* frame and will pass over that *doorway*, and he will not permit the destroyer to enter your houses and strike you down. "Obey these instructions as a lasting ordinance for you and your descendants. When you enter the land that the Lord will give you as he promised, observe this ceremony. and when your children ask you, what does this ceremony mean to you? Then tell them, it is the Passover sacrifice to the Lord, who passed over the houses of the Israelites in Egypt and spared our homes when he struck down the Egyptians." Then the people bow down and worship. The Israelites did just what the Lord commanded Moses and Aaron. At midnight the Lord struck down all the firstborn in Egypt, from the firstborn of pharaoh, who sat on the throne, to the firstborn of the prisoner, who was in the dungeon, and the firstborn of all the livestock as well. Pharaoh, and all his officials and all the Egyptians got up during the night, and there was a loud wailing in all of Egypt, for there was not a house without someone dead.

This group of verses does not directly represent symbology referenced in the title of this chapter about a *doorway* or *doors*. But it does in very graphic terms specify the placing of the lamb's blood on the lintel above and on the side posts of the doorway. There is specific symbology being referenced here, and it certainly does refer directly to our Lord Jesus Christ, the Way, the Truth, and the Life. For within the instructions given by Moses to the Israelites in captivity and the following of the directions given, you were to swipe the hyssop dipped in blood, across the lentil, and down the sides. What inherently is being displayed is the symbology of Jesus, the Lamb of God, and the lamb's blood is referencing to the future where He will be placed on the Cross, typifying and referring to our future salvation by Jesus Christ at the Cross. For in this very manner, all of the Old Testament stories give a reference or typify in some way the character of our Lord Jesus Christ and the heart of His Father collectively, which was recorded and inspired by God Almighty, El Shaddai in scripture.

So after further scrutiny and inspection, this group of scriptures very much speak directly to that *doorway*. In Psalm 24:7, it says:

> Lift up your heads, you Gates: be lifted up, you ancient *doors*, that the King of glory may come in. Who is this King of glory? The Lord strong and mighty, the Lord mighty in battle. Lift up your heads, you Gates; lift them up, you, ancient *doors*, that the King of glory may come in. Who is he, this King of glory? The Lord Almighty—he is the King of glory.

This is an amazing revelation that I am discovering myself as I am unpacking and examining this scripture selection more closely than I have in the past. As it turns out, I may benefit as much out of this book as my readers will. It is possible. What is jumping out at me as I am reexamining this scripture is most revealing. For initially, the direction of this work was to highlight, spotlight, and direct our *doorways* and paths to God.

THERE IS A DOORWAY...

What this scripture is suggesting, upon close reflection, is that in all actuality, He (God) is equally trying to open the *doorways* and lift the *gates* from Him back to us. Wow! What a revelation. This scripture is directly speaking about the hurdles and the blockages of the *doorways* that cause our stumbling. It is in its revelation of messianic concepts, as God commands, that these gates or *doorways* in stumbling be taken out of the way and be opened up.

That is a powerful revelation, for it shows the Father's efforts and nature of His heart in seeking and desiring communion with us too, as well as how He has worked with and in me specifically in this very area. That is what is meant when we say He is a jealous God, not appreciating His glory and worship and credit being given where it ought not to be. In Jeremiah 29:11–14, God is speaking to the returning exiles from Babylon who had disobeyed His ordinances and allowed them to be taken into Babylonian captivity. In a similar storyline to the parable of the prodigal son, this scripture speaks of God's wayward children returning to their homeland and getting back to worship of Jehovah. Jeremiah 29:10–14 says:

> This is what the Lord says: "When 70 years are completed for Babylon, I will come to you and fulfill my good promise to bring you back to this place. For I know the plans I have for you, declares the Lord, plans to prosper you and not to harm you, plans to give you hope and a future. Then you will call on me and come and pray to me and I will listen to you. You will seek me and find me when you seek me with all your heart. I will be found by you, declares the Lord, and will bring you back from captivity."

This is truly what happened to me after a failed relationship of five years, about two and a half years now, almost three years ago. Not having a plan and needing to make a clean break, I had, what would have appeared to, hit my bottom. It was at this point in my predicament that I was basically at a point of loss with no direction, solid purpose, or idea where my life would head and nowhere to live for about three months. It by far had not been the most traumatic event in my life, but it left me the most emotionally bereft I had ever been.

I had fallen down into the emotional "gutter." That is just where He came after me. I got my Bible out, and I have not put it back. In my broken emotional state, I resumed my search for direction, answers and maybe find my purpose in His word, for I knew of no other place where I would find God's wisdom and answers. For even in my lost state, with not a lot of possibilities, I thankfully knew where to go and search for Him and the real answers to help find my way.

God was calling and looking for me just as I was for Him. It has been over these last few years where I have pursued diligently the message contained within His Word, washing and bathing daily in it and studying to understand the new dispensation that we are under that was delivered with Christ's finished work at the Cross. The Law of Grace and Truth and its powerful concepts have been established and revealed through Jesus Christ, and they are unequivocally true, more so than anything I have ever known, completely sewing up all the loose ends and inconsistencies that have plagued my path to a clearer understanding, which praise God has been the fuel of my zeal for the engine that has driven this book. This endeavor has been to transfer, relay, or usher you to the place where these answers to the deepest mysteries of our existence are to be found.

Getting back on point with the theme of this chapter, I'm going to start back in Genesis 4:6–7:

> Then the Lord said to Cain, why are you angry? Why is your face downcast? If you do what is right, will you not be excepted? But if you do not do what is right, sin is crouching at your *door*; he desires to have you, but you must rule over it.

There is a principle in Bible study that is called the first mention. It emphasizes the significance of any specific word, where it is

THERE IS A DOORWAY...

first mentioned in the scriptures. This is the first mention of the word *door*. Upon close inspection, there is more meaning in this scripture than what first meets the eye. It speaks of sin crouching at our *door* and that it desires to have us, and we must rule over it. The scripture is making mention of a *door* here, as the LORD is speaking to Cain in this application.

However, taken out of this context in a broader application, generically, it speaks of a *door* that is before all of us, or Cain in this instance, that leads to somewhere. And this *door* has sin crouching behind it if we do not do what is right. And equally we not must open our *door* to it. Sound words, very applicable, and in this instance, it brings me to point out another concept that appears quite often in Bible study. That is the concept of duality. That is when a story, parable, or message in the Bible is used and applied with the same story happening or repeating itself many generations apart in two different periods. I believe that is exactly what is happening here.

Fairly clear, in this case, where the *LORD* is clearly speaking to Cain in this scripture, and at the same time, it is a message that easily lands with wisdom for all *believers*. The next verse in the Old Testament (Covenant) that we will examine and continue with on the theme of the *door* or the *doorway* is 2 Chronicles 4:19–22 when speaking of the construction of the first temple. There is a reference to the temple furnishings, which I will quote here,

> Solomon also made all the furnishings that were in God's temple: the golden altar; the tables on which was the bread of the Presence the lampstands of pure gold with their lamps, to burn in front of the inner sanctuary as prescribed; The pure gold, wick trimmers, sprinkling bowls, dishes and censers; and the gold *doors* of the temple: the inner *doors* to the Most Holy Place and the *doors* of the main hall.

As I have previously pointed out, there are a good many tools and tips of navigation that help in the journey of reading and understanding the Holy Scriptures. And as we know, the book is full of parables, analogies, and symbology. One of the absolutes that has been revealed through study is that God uses a reference to precious metals when grading or classifying elements of His judicial requirements.

More specifically is that when He uses a reference to gold, the metal, it is the symbol of His divine righteousness. Secondly, and similarly, silver is used when God is referring to redemption, and when He references the metal bronze, it is the symbol for God's judgment. Given that information, we glean through the symbology used in the verses from 2 Chronicles referenced above and from many years of study and good teaching that God's presence resided in the temple, and in the center of the most sacred part of the temple was the mercy seat, which we know is a symbol of Jesus Christ and of God's very own heart, and was hammered out and wrapped completely from one large piece of gold.

For it was God's presence (His Shekinah Glory), that was housed within the mercy seat that was released on that day at Calvary, the moment that Christ expired on the Cross. The curtain, which surrounded the sacred mercy seat (*the Ark of the Covenant*), the Most *Holy of Holies*, was torn in two, all twenty layers, approximately six inches thick, from the ceiling to floor, representing that God's Spirit no longer dwelled with the Hebrew people in the temple only, for they rejected the *Holy One* of Israel with His presence no longer *veiled* from us, as the direct symbology implies.

The golden *doors* symbolize that our entrance into the temple or to the Father God is through the righteousness of Jesus Christ. For our righteousness is given to us freely as a gift from the Father through the Son, not by any works or performance that we may have ever achieved but simply by the fact that *believing in* and excepting the Son whom the Father sent. This scripture may easily be repeated too, possibly even three times in this book because it could almost be assigned easily to any one of the chapters. For it is with the repetitiveness and the continued hearing of the word of God that your *faith* is increased and your knowledge grows.

THERE IS A DOORWAY...

It is through the learning and understanding of the scriptures that we are then able to more correctly walk with our Lord, and He can continue to shed His *Grace* on us. Right in line with this thought is a very apt scripture from Romans 5:20, which sheds light on this, and it says, "The Law was brought in, so that the trespass might increase. But where sin increased, *Grace* increased all-the-more." What this affirms in this scripture is that in our weaknesses, God is made stronger and is attracted to our weaknesses (His Grace), which we can overcome through Him.

Through His love for us, His *Grace* (or unmerited favor or undeserved kindness), is what He sheds upon us, and superabounds for those that *believe* in the Son whom the Father sent to take away the sins of the world. As God's word says, "We cannot approach or commune with God until we know He exists, and we have a desire and need for Him." Also, that "He is a rewarder of those that earnestly, or diligently, seek Him." Now back on track with our *doorway* scriptures.

There is something I would like to address here that could have been inserted before. However, since we are moving along a progression of the accumulation of Bible knowledge, it will work just nicely here. From the *Zondervan New Compact Bible Dictionary*, I have selected to insert here the definition they have for the word *door*, "Door, in ancient times, turned on pivots, turning into sockets above and below, and were frequently two-leaved."

The word is often used in the New Testament in a figurative sense, many times referring to Christ (John 10:2, 7 and Revelation 3:20), but also to opportunity (Matthew 25:10, Acts 14: 7, and 1 Corinthians 16:9) and freedom and power (Colossians 4:3). First, we will look at the scriptures offered in the concordance from above that deal with Christ's divinity or deity. That is of all the ones offered in the concordances referred to in the scriptures. In John 10:1, we will start to examine the concept of the *door*; here, however, although meaning the same thing, it is called a *gate*.

Oddly enough, this scripture again is quite similar to some we came across earlier and have a dual usage in the structure of their storyline. Here, specifically in this chapter and group of scriptures, it deals simultaneously with both the good shepherd and the *gate* or *doorway* to the sheep pen, consequently capturing two of our chapter subjects in one parable. Praise God. John 10:1–10 says:

> "Very truly I tell you Pharisees, anyone who does not enter into the sheep pen by the *gate*, but climbs in some other way, is a thief and a robber. The one who enters by the *gate* is the Shepherd of the sheep. The *gatekeeper* opens the *gate* for him, and the sheep listen to his voice. He calls his own sheep by name and leads them out. When he has brought out all his own, he goes on ahead of them, and his sheep follow him because they know his voice. But they will never follow a stranger; in fact, they will run away from him because they do not recognize a stranger's voice." Jesus used this figure of speech, but the Pharisees did not understand what he was telling them. Therefore, Jesus said again, "Very truly I tell you, I am the *gate* for the sheep. All who have come before me are thieves and robbers, but the sheep had not listened to them. I am the *gate*; whoever enters through me will be saved. They will come in, and go out, and find pasture. The thief comes only to steal and kill and destroy; I have come that they may have life and have it to the full."

I do not think it requires me going out on a limb here, and there is not much for me to delineate. I believe, even with the basic knowledge of the Bible, these scriptures here speak well for themselves. Now, moving to the scriptures proffered above in the book of Revelation, beginning with the one in Revelation 3:19–22:

> Those whom I love I rebuke and discipline. Still be Earnest and repent. Here I am! I stand at the *door* and knock. If anyone hears my voice and

> opens the *door*, I will come in and eat with that person, and they with me. To the one who is victorious, I will give the right to sit with me on my throne, just as I was victorious and sat down with my father on his throne. Whoever has the ears, let them hear what the Holy Spirit says to the churches.

Here again, my task is not very difficult. For the scriptures here and the Bible in general, while they may have some complex concepts and explanations of our mysterious God's mighty plans, they are written to us in a way for us to understand. However, this may take some familiarity and call for a depth of study. But I tell you this, God's word is true, and that is what has been revealed to me by the Holy Spirit and to which I solemnly affirm, after much searching and continued study for nearly three years now of a daily bathing in His word.

Now moving to a scripture in Isaiah referencing a mention of a *door*, we go to 45:1–9:

> This is what the LORD says to his anointed, to Cyrus, whose right hand, I take hold of and subdue nations before him and to strip kings of their armor, and to open *doors* before him. So that *Gates* will not be shut: I will go before you and will level the mountains; I will break down the gates of bronze and cut through bars of iron. I will give you hidden treasures, which is stored in secret places, so that you may know that I am the LORD, the God of Israel, who summons you by name. For the sake of Jacob my servant, of Israel my chosen, I summon you by name and bestow on you a title of honor, and though you do not acknowledge me. I am the Lord, and there is no other; apart from me, there is no God. I will strengthen you though you have not acknowledged me, so that from the rising of the sun to the place of its setting. People may know there

is none besides me. I am the LORD, and there is no other. I formed the light and create darkness, I bring prosperity and create disaster; I, the LORD does all these things. "You heavens above, rain down my righteousness; let the clouds shower it down. Let the earth opened wide, let salvation spring up, let righteousness flourish with it; I, the LORD, have created it. "Woe to those who quarrel with their Maker, those who are nothing but potsherds among the potsherds on the ground. Does the clay say to the Potter, what are you making? Does your work say, the Potter has no hands?

This book of Isaiah was written approximately 800 BC. This prediction (prophecy) in the book of Isaiah occurs some 200 to 250 years prior to these events taking place that name Cyrus. As I just stated, nearly 200 years in advance of a prophesied prediction that was completely fulfilled to every "jot and tittle." Accurately. After reading these scriptures, I am prayerful that you are grasping the profoundness of these Old Testament prophecies.

This is ultimately miraculous by our world standards but not for God. For one-third of this Bible is prophecy. That reveals one-third of the writings of the book of the Holy Scriptures are projected forward in future prophecies. Of this fact, I cannot emphasize enough here how important and integral that this facet of prophecy is ultimately in the discerning and understanding of God's complete salvation plan for us. Coupled with the fact that God made time and exists outside of His created construct, as well as knowing it backward and forward. Amen.

That is likely to be the subject for my next book, and it is too much of a layered and involved topic to venture into here. It is for another time. The next verse we will examine is in the book of Isaiah also 26:20–21:

Go, my people, and into your rooms and shut the *doors* behind you; hide yourselves for a little while, until his wrath has passed by. See, the Lord is coming out of his dwelling to punish the people of the earth for their sins. The earth will disclose the bloodshed on it; the earth will conceal its slain no longer.

This prophecy given by God to Isaiah is a declaration of God Almighty pointing toward the latter days and the coming wrath. When the unbelievers, which include the people of Israel, or the Jewish people, and others, who have denied the visitation of our Lord and Savior Jesus Christ, and crucified Him, the Messiah, and their contribution to His denial and rejection. God's Word to us in the Holy Bible was never intended to be anything but a divinely inspired "owner's manual" from our Father, to us, explaining the plan for our salvation and chronicling the walk of the Father God with his "chosen, stubborn, obstinate, and stiff-necked people."

It chronicles and documents the history of His chosen people Israel, which became the vehicle that delivers the Messiah and eventually all the spiritual descendants of Abraham and physical descendants as well, who also are saved by God's *Grace through our Faith* in our Savior, sent from God Himself. It says in Genesis 22:7–8 a magnanimous verse where Isaac asks his father, who is being tested by God.

> Isaac spoke up and said to his father Abraham, "Father? "Yes, my son?" Abraham replied. "The fire and the wood are here, Isaac said, but where is the lamb for the burnt offering?" Abraham answered, "God himself will provide the lamb for the burnt offering, my son."

At this point in the book, I hope you caught that. That last scripture presents the concept of dual occurrences or what is referred to as the micro and macro viewpoints of the Bible. For this very scripture carries within it in one sentence God's purpose, plan for us, and our salvation program, all contained in this one most profound scripture from the heart and mind of our Almighty God, "God himself will provide the lamb for the burnt offering my Son."

It will be very difficult to provide a more consequential, monumental, and declarative statement from the mouth of our God. Firming this up in case it may have been missed or that your familiarity of Old Testament scripture and prophecy is still being developed, this story on Abraham's testing of his *Faith* by God, to see if he had *believed* what God had revealed to him of his future, is a direct typification of our Father God's surrendering of His *only* Son for the redemption plan God has instituted through Jesus Christ the Messiah, the only begotten Son of the Father.

His (God's) request of him (Abraham) was a semblance of God's own heart being revealed to us here, establishing these events that our great God is never one to ask us something he would not or that he did not already do himself. When I first realized this very fact, it carried quite a resonance of His power with me directly. I was somewhere around thirty-five or forty years of age and had worked many jobs, some union, some nonunion, in construction and in many other walks of life.

One thing had revealed itself many times over the course of these years under managerial leadership in the positions that I held. That primary factor that continued to reveal itself was this, that the best bosses or leaders that I had ever served under were well-rounded individuals mentally, and one standard of performance had revealed itself, among the good ones that I had. And that one trait was this. That there was never a *good* boss or leader that would ask or inquire of you to do something, or even anything, that they themselves were not willing to do or that they hadn't done at one time or another themselves.

For not only was this a test of Abraham's *Faith*, but God was simultaneously foreshadowing and foreordaining His plan for our redemption that was necessary after Adam's disobedience and the direct cause of our fallen nature and our need for a salvation plan. This gargantuan fact of knowledge about our God has almost singlehandedly convinced me of His nature, His love for us, and His ultimate divinity, of which I no longer question, and it is the quest of this book to help to deliver you to that same point of understanding. Jumping off the *doorway scriptures* there for a bit, but now returning, although there definitely was a pertinent and edifying message there.

Initially, I did a large dive into researching every scripture in the Bible that spoke of or dealt with *doorways*. Prior to this point in this chapter, I have followed the flow of the Spirit's direction of scriptures chosen, used, and explained. After quoting a powerful scripture in James, I am at this point going to redirect the order of the selected scriptures and to work methodically from Matthew on in the New Covenant (Testament) using a rapid-fire method of saturation that works most effectively in establishing an indelible picture message that is the very method God employs in the Holy Scriptures in His effort to convey or transfer knowledge and critical information of Him to us in His Word.

It is by design, for I have been riding on the Lord's shoulders during this entire time that I have been in composition of this proclamation that has been called forth of me by the Holy Spirit. James 4:4–6 says clearly,

> You adulterous people, don't you know that friendship with the world is enmity against God. Therefore, anyone who chooses to be a friend of the world is an enemy of God. Or do you think scripture says without reason that He, (God) longingly, and jealously longs for the Spirit that he has caused to dwell in us? But he gives us more *Grace*. That is why scripture says; God opposes the proud, but shows favor, (Grace, Mercy, Undeserved Kindness) to the humble.

I wanted to insert this scripture here specifically for the purpose of bearing out the concept of God's of pre-seeding in our being those specific traits of our awareness of Him and how strongly we are drawn to His will and to His purposes, proving by scripture from His word that our callings to Him are by His design and from Him and how the *great spiritual* mind of all has ordered all of these things into existence and is still in complete, and I mean complete, control.

In Matthew 23:2–15, it gives a reference to a *door*, but much is revealed just prior to that of God's chosen people Israel, under Mosaic Law, and also instruction to His other flock, those of us that have been saved by His Grace through our Faith in Christ Jesus.

> The teachers of the Law and the Pharisees sit in Moses' seat. So you must be careful to do anything they tell you. But do not do what they do, for they do not practice what they preach. They tie up heavy cumbersome loads and put them on other peoples shoulders, but they themselves are not willing to lift a finger to move them. Everything they do is done for people to see; They make their phylacteries wide and the tassels on their garments long; they love the place of honor at banquets and the most important seats in the synagogues; they love to be greeted with respect in the marketplaces and to be called "Rabbi" by others. But you are not to be called 'Rabbi', for you have one teacher, and you are all brothers. And do not call anyone on earth "Father", for you have one Father, and He is in Heaven. Nor are you to be called instructors, for you have one instructor, the Messiah. The greatest among you will be your servant. For those who exalt themselves will be humbled, and those who humble themselves will be exalted. Woe to you teachers of the Law and Pharisees, you hypocrites! You shut the *door* of the kingdom of heaven in peoples faces. You yourselves do not enter, nor will you let those enter that are trying to. Woe to you, teachers of the Law and Pharisees, you hypocrites! You travel over land and sea to win a single convert, and when you have succeeded, you make them twice as much a child of hell as you are.

And skip down in the same chapter now to verses 37–39:

> Jerusalem, Jerusalem, you who kill the prophets and stone those sent to you, how often I longed to gather your children together, as a hen gathers her chicks under her wings, and you were not willing. Look, your house is left to you desolate. For I tell you, you will not see me again until you say, "Blessed is he who comes in the name of the Lord."

These scriptures just cited here are pointing out to the Hebrew people just how badly they missed His message, word, *Grace*, and their role in any and all of that. Not only that but also who the Messiah was, His role, and what it could have meant to them if they would have been able to receive it. But they were full of self-pride and self-righteousness, erring in the belief that their performance of said Laws was yielding them their salvation before God, and it was not on their performance but on the atoning of and cleansing blood of the sacrificed animal that would have forwarded their righteous standing as a forerunner or a pre-type of the ultimate sacrificial lamb supplied for us all, Jesus Christ, and not from their beliefs that they were righteous by their performing of the works of the law.

Continuing in Matthew 24:30–44 where the next *door* usage I am selecting is this:

> Then will appear the sign of the son of man in heaven. And then all the peoples of earth will mourn when they see the Son of man coming on the clouds of heaven, with power and great glory. And he will send his Angels with the loud trumpet call, and they will gather his elect from the 4 winds, from one end of the heavens to the other. Now learn this lesson from the fig tree: as soon as it's twigs get tender and its leaves come out, you know that summer is near. Even so, when you

> see all these things, you know if that it is near, right at the *door*. Truly I tell you, this generation will certainly not pass away until all these things have happened. Heaven and earth will pass away, but my words will never pass away. Of that day and hour, no one knows, not even the son, but only the Father. As it was in the days of Noah, so it will be at the coming of the son of man. In the days before the flood, people were eating and drinking, marrying and giving in marriage, up to the day Noah entered the ark; and they knew nothing about what would happen until the flood came and took them all away. That is how it will be at the coming of the Son of Man. Two men will be in the field; one will be taken and the other left. Two women will be grinding with a hand mill; one will be taken and the other one left. Therefore keep watch, because you do not know on what day your Lord will come. But understand this: If the owner of the house had known at what time of the night the thief was coming, he would have kept watch and not have let his house be broken into. So you must be ready, because the Son of Man will come at an hour when you do not expect him.

Now in chapter 25, still in Matthew, we pick up another door-referencing scripture to examine. A parable in Matthew 25:1–13 says:

> At that time the kingdom of heaven will be like ten virgins who took their lamps and went out to meet the bridegroom. Five of them were foolish and five were wise. The foolish ones took their lamps but did not take any oil with them. The wise ones, however, took oil in jars along

> with their lamps. The bridegroom was a long time in coming, and they all became drowsy and fell asleep. At midnight the cry rang out: Here's the bridegroom! Come out to meet him! Then all the virgins woke up and trimmed their lamps. The foolish ones said to the wise, give us some of your oil; our lamps are going out. No, they replied, there may not be enough for both us and you. Instead, go to those who sell oil and buy some for yourself. but while they were on their way to buy the oil, the bridegroom arrived. The virgins who are ready went in with him to the wedding banquet. And the *door* was shut. later the others also came Lord, Lord, they said open the *door* for us! but he replied truly I tell you, I don't know you therefore keep watch, because you do not know the day or the hour.

Moving into the chapter of Mark, there are a couple subtle *door* references that are speaking directly on *Faith*, and in my estimation, that is the reason the detail is mentioned as we must not forget God is magnificently clever, and given that we now know there are no insignificant details in the Bible. In Mark 1:33 and again in Mark 2:1–12, we are informed in these recurring themes that suggest that healings, enlightenment, the bread of life, salvation, eternity with God, everything offered to us is on the other side of that *door*, and *Faith* in Jesus Christ will get you through it and to Him. First in Mark 1:29–34, then even more clearly in Mark 2:1–12 and Mark 1:29–34:

> As soon as they left the synagogue they went with James and John to the home of Simon and Andrew. Simon's Mother-in-law was in bed with a fever, and they immediately told Jesus about her. So he went to her, took her hand and helped her up. The fever left Her and she began to wait

on them. That evening after sunset the people brought to Jesus all the sick and demon possessed. The whole town gathered at the *door* and Jesus healed many demons, but he would not let the demons speak, because they knew who he was.

And here's the second of the two scriptures we are discussing here, Mark 2:1–12:

A few days later, when Jesus again entered Capernaum, the people heard that he had come home. They gathered in such large numbers that there was no room left, not even outside the *door*, and he preached the word to them. Some men came, bringing to him a paralyzed man, carried by four of them. Since they could not get him to Jesus because of the crowd, they made an opening in the roof above Jesus by digging through it and then lowered the mat the man was lying on. When Jesus saw their *Faith*, he said to the paralyzed man, son, your sins are forgiven. Now some teachers of the Law were sitting there, thinking to themselves, why does this fellow talk like that? He's blaspheming! Who can forgive sins but God alone? Immediately Jesus knew in his spirit that this was what they were thinking in their hearts, and he said to them, why are you thinking these things? Which is easier to say to this paralyzed man, your sins are forgiven, or to say get up, take your mat and walk? But I want you to know that the son of man has authority on earth to forgive sins. So he said to the man, I tell you get up take your mat and go home. He got up, took his mat and walked out in full view of them all. This amazed everyone and they praised God, saying we have never seen anything like this.

THERE IS A DOORWAY...

Faith is going through the *door*.

It's going to get a little heavier now as we venture into some prophetic scriptures that reference the *doorway* and deliver some timely and powerfully pertinent information quite in line with the purpose and objectives of this book. Mark 13 is just such a wheelbarrow full of the most valuable knowledge of God's plan. Since we have seen that God's word is discernable, with continued study, and that it is written to us and it is for us, it stands then that He has written it to us, for us, to receive His word on all things of consequence without a PhD. By comparing scripture with scripture and building on a foundation of sound doctrine and where and when necessary, seeking assistance from credible Bible sources, you will see why I have prefaced this so deeply once we move into the examining of this specific group of scriptures, again containing our targeted reference on *doorways*. Mark 13:1–36, the whole chapter, says:

> As Jesus was leaving the temple, one of his disciples said to him, "Look teacher what massive stones!" "What magnificent buildings!" Do you see all these great buildings? Replied Jesus. Not one stone will be left on another; every one will be thrown down. As Jesus was sitting on the Mount of Olives opposite the temple, Peter, James, John and Andrew asked him privately, Tell us when will these things happen? And what will be the sign that they are all about to be fulfilled? Jesus said to them: watch out that no one deceives you. many will come in my name, claiming I am he, and will deceive many. When you hear of wars and rumors of wars, do not be alarmed. such things must happen, but the end is still to come. Nation will rise against nation, and kingdom against kingdom. There will be earthquakes in various places, and famines. these are the beginning of birth pains. You must be on your guard. You will be handed over to the

local councils and flogged in the synagogues. On account of me you will stand before governors in Kings as witnesses to them and the gospel must first be preached to all nations. Whenever you are arrested and brought to trial, do not worry beforehand about what to say. Just say whatever is given you at the time, for it is not you speaking, but the Holy Spirit. Brother will betray brother to death and the father his child. Children will rebel against their parents and have them put to death. Everyone will hate you because of me, but the one who stands firm till the end will be saved. When you see the abomination that causes desolation standing where it does not belong—let the reader understand—Then let those who are in Judea flee to the mountains. let no one on the housetop go down or enter the house to take anything out. let no one in the field go back to get their cloak. How dreadfully will be in those days for pregnant women and nursing mothers! Pray that this will not take place in winter, because those will be days of distress unequalled from the beginning, when God created the world, until now—and never be equaled again. But for the sake of the elect. At that time if anyone says to you, 'Look, here is the Messiah!' or, 'Look, there he is!' Do not believe it. For false messiahs and false prophets will appear and perform signs and wonders to deceive, if possible, even the elect. So be on your guard; I have told you everything ahead of time. But in those days, following that distress, the sun will be darkened, and the moon will not give its light; and the stars will fall from the sky, and the heavenly bodies will be shaken. At that time people will see the Son of Man coming in the clouds with power and great glory. And

THERE IS A DOORWAY...

> He will send his angels to gather his elect from the four winds, from the ends of the earth to the ends of the heavens. "Now learn this lesson of the fig tree: As soon as its twigs get tender and its leaves come out, you know that summer is near. Even so, when you see these things happening, you know that it is near, right at the *door*. Truly I tell you, this generation will certainly not pass away until all these things have happened. Heaven and earth will pass away, but my words will never pass away. But about that day or hour no one knows, not even the angels in heaven, nor the Son, but only the Father. Be on guard! Be alert! You do not know when that time will come. It's like a man going away: He leaves his house and puts his servants in charge, each with their assigned task, and tells the one at the *door* to keep watch. Therefore keep watch because you do not know when the owner of the house will come back—whether in the evening, or at midnight, or when the rooster crows, or at dawn. If he comes suddenly, do not let him find you sleeping. What I say to you, I say to everyone: *Watch!*"

Clearly, Jesus is at the other side of the *door*, or *doorway*, itself. He is the good shepherd of us, His sheep, and also, Jesus Christ is the very *Grace* of God. We move now in our progression into the book of Luke 11:5–13. Jesus is explaining some godly insights on prayer, worship, and love. Most worthy of examining and reflection, it includes a couple of references to the *door*.

> Then Jesus said to them "Suppose you have a friend, and you go to him in the middle of the night and say, friend, lend me 3 loaves of bread; a friend of mine on a journey has come to me, and I have no food to offer him. And suppose the

one inside answers, don't bother me. The *door* is already locked and my children and I are in bed. I can't get up and give you anything. I tell you, even though he will not get up and give you the bread because of friendship, yet because of your shameless audacity he will surely get up and give you as much as you need. So, I say to you, "Ask and it will be given to you; Seek and you will find; Knock and the *door* will be opened to you. For everyone who asks receives; The one who seeks finds; And to the one who knocks, the *door* will be opened. Which of you fathers, if your son asks for a fish, will give him a snake instead? Or if he asks for an egg, will you give him a scorpion? If you then, though you are evil, know how to give good gifts to your children, how much more will your father in heaven give the Holy Spirit to those who ask him!"

Now, picking this next specific scripture in Luke 12:35–40:

Be dressed ready for service and keep your lamps burning, like servants waiting for their master to return from a wedding banquet, so that when he comes and knocks, they can immediately open the *door* for him. It will be good for those servants whose master finds them watching when he comes. Truly I tell you, he will dress himself to serve, and will have them recline at the table and will come and wait on them. It will be good for those servants whose master finds them ready, even if he comes in the middle of the night or toward Daybreak. But understand this, if the owner of the house had known at what hour the thief was coming, he would not have let his house be broken into. You also must be ready, because

THERE IS A DOORWAY...

> the Son of Man will come at an hour when you do not expect Him.

So again, clearly in the usage of the *doorway* reference and analogy, it is clear who is the *door* and what is on the other side of it. This is without a doubt one of the most elemental and primary concepts of God and, at the same time, the totality of all wisdom and knowledge and the sum-total of our complete existence and our reality at the very same time—Jesus Christ. For effect, I am selecting for comparison and analysis two profound scriptures, one at the beginning of Genesis 1 and the other in the beginning of the book of the Gospel of John to bear out my last conclusive statements. Genesis 1:26–31 and 2:1 says:

> Then God said, let us make mankind in our image, in our likeness, so that they may rule over the fish in the sea and the birds in the Sky, over the livestock and all the wild animals, and over all the creatures that move along the ground. So God created mankind in his own image, in the image of God he created them; Male and female he created them. God blessed them and said to them, be fruitful and the increase in number; Fill the earth and subdue it. Rule over the fish in the sea and the birds in the sky and over every living creature that moves on the ground. Then God said I give you every seed-bearing plant on the face of the whole earth and every tree that has fruit with seeds in it they will be yours for food. And to all the beasts of the earth and all the birds in the sky and all the creatures that move along the ground everything that has a breath of life in it. I give every green plant for food. And it was so. God saw all that he had made, and it was very good. And there was evening, and there was

morning the 6th day. Thus the heavens and the earth were completed in all their vast array.

And now, the second of the two, from the very beginning of the Gospel of John 1:1–14:

> In the beginning was the Word, and the Word was with God, and the Word was God. He was with God in the beginning. Through him all things were made; Without him nothing was made that has been made. In him was life, in that life was the light of all mankind. The light shines in the darkness, and the darkness has not overcome it. There was a man sent from God whose name was John. He came as a witness to testify concerning that light, so that through him all might believe. He himself was not that light; He came only as a witness to the light. The true light that gives light to everyone was coming into the world. He was in the world, and though the world was made through him, the world did not recognize him. He came to that which was his own, but his own did not receive him. Yet to all who did receive him, to those who believed in his name, he gave the right to become children of God—Children born not of natural descent, nor of human decision, or a husband's will, but born of God. The Word became flesh and made his dwelling among us. We have seen his glory, the glory of the one and only son, who came from the Father, full of *Grace* and Truth.

Now jumping to verses 17–18 and continuing:

> For the Law was given through Moses; *Grace* and Truth came through Jesus Christ. No

> one has ever seen God, but the one and only son, who is himself God and is in closest relationship with the Father, has made him known.

These scriptures enumerate the power, majesty, and divine control of our loving Father, His creation, and the ultimate, righteous, and just outcome that He has orchestrated over the long haul, which facilitates a plan for us with eternity in heaven, with our great God and us, His *faithful* and compassionate and redeemed, forgiven children. Fulfilling His desire for such, as He has revealed it to us from front to back, through His Word, our Holy Bible.

I feel that what I have been called to share and point to in God's Holy Word is His overall plan for humanity, our redemption, and our eternal salvation. Our mighty God, Lord and Savior, Father, Son, and His Holy Spirit have now been spotlighted, as they have come to me, in my search for understanding through the revelation of the Word and no other way. For me, it is amazing that this calling sparked and inspired my renewed interest or search into God's Word and that He delivered to me where the real answers are found.

And I am so thankful to God that He did. I felt that I had to share what has made me a changed man. As we begin to move toward the close of this book, I have selected several more *doorway*-related scriptures and stacked them for flow, information contained, and importance of knowledge delivered.

There are two scriptures in John's Gospel referencing our *doors* topic. Following here and beginning with the first in John 20:19–23, its paragraph specific title is "Jesus Appears to His Disciples,"

> On the evening of that first day of the week, when the disciples were together, with the *doors* locked for fear of the Jewish leaders, Jesus came and stood among them and said, peace be with you. After he said this, he showed them his hands, inside the disciples were overjoyed when they saw the Lord. Again Jesus said, peace be with you as the Father has sent me, I am sending you. And

with that he breathed on them and said, receive the Holy Spirit. if you forgive anyone sins, their sins are forgiven; If you do not forgive them, they are not forgiven.

Now, continuing in John 20:24–29:

> Now Thomas (also known as Didymus) one of the twelve, was not with the disciples when Jesus came. So the other disciples told him, we have seen the Lord! But he said to them, "Unless I see the nail marks in his hands and put my finger where the nails were, and put my hand into his side, I will not believe." A week later his disciples were in the house again, and Thomas was with them. Though the *doors* were locked, Jesus came and stood among them and said, "Peace be with you"! Then he said to Thomas, "Put your finger here; See my hands. Reach out your hand and put it into my side. Stop doubting and *believe.*" Thomas said to him, my Lord and my God! Then Jesus told him, because you have seen me you have *believed*; "Blessed are those who have not seen and yet have *believed.*"

It is very interesting how these two scriptures are set up. With both scenarios speaking of Jesus's disciples gathered in the "upper room," which is mentioned like every seemingly unimportant detail, because as we have learned, there are no insignificant details in the Bible. For it is the inspired, breathed, and written words of our El Shaddai, God Almighty. More specifically, in both instances, the disciples are locked in for fear of the Jews. We know they are *faithful believers*, and by their *Faith*, He, Jesus, is in their presence, as their *Faith* draws Him to them, even though it appears they are isolated and alone, but they are not, are they? I suggest that *Faith* is also the majestic *doorway*.

THERE IS A DOORWAY...

The Lord sees our Faith as us knocking on His *door*. For our Lord and Savior is drawn to and made complete by our sinful nature and our awareness of our need for Him, in Jesus Christ, the Messiah, and the forgiveness included by Grace because of our Faith in Him. It was because of their *Faith*, their *belief* in the one and only Son of God sent to redeem freely all who will *believe*. The next scripture in this progression of *doorway* references is in Acts, and it couldn't apply better or fit more aptly than here, just after the two previous scripture verses in John. Acts 14:21–28 says:

> They preached the gospel in that city and won a large number of disciples. Then they returned to Lystra, Iconium and Antioch, strengthening the disciples and encouraging them to remain true to the Faith. We must go through many hardships to enter the Kingdom of God, they said. Paul and Barnabas appointed elders for them in each church and, with prayer and fasting, committed them to the Lord, and whom they had put their trust. After going through Pisidia they came into Pamphylia, and when they had preached the word in Perga, they went down to Attalia. From Attalia, they sailed back to Antioch, where they had been committed to the *Grace* of God for the work they had now completed. On arriving there, they gathered the church together and reported all that God had done through them and how he had opened a *door* of *Faith* to the gentiles. And they stayed there a long time with the disciples.

God's word is built, verse upon verse, scripture upon scripture. This is how we must proceed in the study and building of understanding of God's Word. For iron sharpens iron, and we must scrutinize and test all beliefs and findings by His every word to be certain of accurate digestion. This verse clearly demonstrates in scripture the very concept that we were exploring and examining in those last scriptures in John.

That scripture in Acts 14 says it just as plain as can be. This helps establish with some concrete doctrine and understanding that you do not need a PhD to understand the Bible. God has made it for us to be able to discern His truths, and not be taught of worldly learned men. I assert that if you diligently seek, God will help you find, just as He has me. His promises are true, and His word never comes back devoid or empty, without a yield. Paul's writings in Corinthians are where we land in our winding down of the "There Is A Doorway" chapter.

As I only have a few of the specific usages left in concluding this final chapter from my research of all the instances in the Bible where it has been employed, most, where applicable, were used. Only in a few instances, they were not pertinent to contribute to our intended objective and were not included. In 1 Corinthians 16:5–9, it gives more clarity on this theme also:

> After I go through Macedonia, I will come to you—I will be going through Macedonia. Perhaps I will stay with you for a while, or even spend the winter, so that you can help me on my journey, wherever I go. For I do not want to see you now and make only a passing visit: I hope to spend some time with you, if the Lord permits. But I will stay on at Ephesus until Pentecost, because a great *door* for effective work has opened to me. And there are many who oppose me.

Its usage is clear and apparent. He is speaking of a *door* opening for the spreading of the Gospel of "being saved by *Grace through Faith* in Jesus Christ and Him crucified, risen on the third day, as He now sits at the right hand of the Father," interceding for us as our eternal High Priest, before the Father, as He has already made the atonement for "all" of our sins.

THERE IS A DOORWAY...

The quote marks in the scripture here were added from me. It says in the second book of Corinthians 2:12–17:

> Now when I went to Troas to preach the Gospel of Christ and found that the Lord had opened a *door* for me, I still had no peace of mind, because I did not find my brother Titus there. So, I said goodbye to them and went on to Macedonia. But thanks be to God, who always leads us as captives in Christ's triumphal procession and uses us to spread the aroma of Christ among those who are being saved and those who are perishing. To the one we are the aroma that brings death; to the other, an aroma that brings life. And who is equal to such a task? Unlike so many, we do not peddle the Word of God for profit. On the contrary, in Christ we speak before God with sincerity, as those sent from God.

Again, there is no mysterious, covert, or hidden meaning here but rather straightforward and sound doctrine and knowledge of our great God and Father, delivered for us through Paul, received by the Holy Spirit of His Son, Christ Jesus. There is a *doorway* to *Faith* in God. That *doorway* is Jesus Christ. We must believe in Him (Christ Jesus) and in His power for it to be enacted in our lives more abundantly.

This last section is a mix of Old and New Testament (Covenant) scripture verses that I have selected as the Holy Spirit has led with purpose, strategy, and direction intended for any and all understanding that I have hopefully been able to help you attain or aspire to attain. In Habakkuk 2:1–4, the Lord's prophet makes some glaring statements, out of the old dispensation, that completely lines up with the new.

Habakkuk 2:1–4 says:

> I will stand at my watch and station myself on the ramparts; I will look to see what he will say to

> me, and what answer I am to give to this complaint. "The Lord's Answer" Then the Lord replied: Write down the revelation and make it plain on tablets so that a herald may run with it. For the revelation awaits an appointed time; It speaks of the end and will not prove false. Though it linger, wait for it; it will certainly come and will not delay. See, the enemy is puffed up; his desires are not upright, but the righteous person will live by his *faithfulness*.

This is the same concept God revealed to Abraham "For Abraham *believed* God, and it was counted to him as righteousness," just as it says in Genesis 15:4–6:

> Then the Word of the Lord came to Him: "This man will not be your heir, but a son who is your own flesh and blood will be your heir." He took him outside and said, "Look up at the sky and count the stars—if you can count them." Then He said to him, "So shall your offspring be." Abraham *believed* the LORD, and it was counted to him as righteousness.

This is the Gospel of God's *Grace* and has been with us and was His eventual plan from the beginning of creation and that God wants us to take Him at His Word and *believe*. The Law was the previous Covenant that God used to establish what sin is and what His (God's) righteousness is also. As we move into our last group of *doorway* scriptures, which appropriately are found in the book written by the Apostle John, in the Revelation, these will obviously be most profound and consequential.

First, in Revelation 3:7–13, which is written to the "Church in Philadelphia":

> To the angel of the Church of Philadelphia write: These are the words of Him that is holy

and true, who holds the key of David. What he opens no one can shut, and what he shuts no one can open. I know your deeds. See I have placed before you an open *door* that no one can shut. I know that you have little strength, yet you have kept my Word and have not denied my name. I will make those who are a synagogue of Satan, who claimed to be Jews though they are not, but are liars—I will make them come and fall-down at your feet and acknowledge that I have loved you. Since you have kept my command to endure patiently, I will also keep you from the hour of trial that is going to come on the whole world to test the inhabitants of the earth. I am coming soon. Hold onto what you have, so that no one will take your crown. The one who is victorious I will make a pillar in the temple of my God. Never again will they leave it. I will write on them the new name of my God and the name of the city of my God, the new Jerusalem, which is coming down out of heaven from my God; And I will also write on them my new name. Whoever has ears, let them hear what the spirit says to the churches.

These verses speak directly to the importance and understanding of prophecy. They speak of voluminous events that will take place up to and during the great tribulation, prophesied to come on all the earth in the latter days. We will fear not, for we have not been saved unto wrath, just as His word clearly says in 1 Thessalonians 5:9–11:

> For He has not appointed us to suffer wrath but to receive salvation through our Lord Jesus Christ. He died for us so that whether we are awake or asleep, we may live together with Him. Therefore encourage one another and build one another up, just as in fact you are doing.

We are down now to our final two scriptures pertaining to the *doorway* references and inferences, starting with one in Revelation 4:1–8:

> After this I looked and there was a *door* standing open to heaven. And the voice I had first heard speaking to me like a trumpet said, "Come up here and I will show you what must take place after this." At once I was in the spirit, and there before me was a throne in heaven with someone sitting on it. And the one who sat there had the appearance of jasper and ruby. A rainbow that shone like an emerald encircled the throne. Surrounding the throne were twenty-four other thrones, and, seated on them were twenty-four elders. They were dressed in white and had crowns of gold on their heads. From the throne came flashes of lightning, rumblings and peals of thunder. In front of the throne, seven lamps were blazing. These are the seven spirits of God. Also in the front of the throne there was what looked like a sea of glass, clear as crystal. In the center around the throne, were four living creatures, and they were covered with eyes, in front and in back. The first living creature was like a lion, the second was like an ox, the third had the face like a man, the fourth was like a flying eagle. Each of the four living creatures had six wings and was covered with eyes all around, even under its wings. Day and night they never stop saying
>
> "Holy, holy, holy is the
> Lord God Almighty, who was, and is,
> And is to come."

THERE IS A DOORWAY...

For a better description of the throne room of heaven, there is not one. The *door* standing before the throne of heaven again is Jesus Christ. For no one can get to the Father unless it is given to him by the Son. And no one can get to the Son unless it is given him by the Father. For Jesus Himself said, "If you have seen me, you have seen the Father, for I and my Fathers purpose are one," which is just as it says in God's promise to us in John 14:8–14:

> Phillip said, "Lord show us the Father and that will be enough for us." Jesus answered, "Don't you know me Phillip, even after I have been among you such a long time? Anyone who has seen me has seen the Father. How can you say, 'Show us the Father'? Don't you *believe* that I am in the Father, and the Father is in me? The words I speak to you I do not speak on my own authority. Rather, it is the Father, living in me, who is doing His work. *Believe* me when I say I am in the Father and the Father is in me; or at least *believe* on the evidence of the works themselves. Very truly I tell you, whoever *believes* in me will do the works I have been doing, and they will do even greater things than these, because I am going to the Father. And I will do whatever you ask in my name, so that the Father may be glorified in the Son. You may ask for anything in my name, and I will do it."

There is no need for interpretation in these verses. It's very straightforward, as I had asked in Jesus's name for God to assist me in this endeavor, and I have felt led and assisted by the power of the Lord in this effort to glorify Him and His Word and that He has seen me through the whole way. God's Word unequivocally means everything that it states. There is no more mystery here. Praise God. In closing, with the last reference to the *doorway*, or *gates* in this instance, near the end of the book of Revelation in 22:14–17, it most profoundly says:

> Blessed are those who wash their robes, that they may have a right to the tree of life and may go through the *gates* into the city. Outside are the dogs, those who practice magic arts, the sexually immoral, the murderers, the idolaters and everyone one who loves and practices falsehood. I, Jesus, have sent my angel to give you this testimony for the churches. I am the root and the offspring of David, and the bright and Morning Star. The spirit and the bride say, "Come!" And let the one who hears say, "Come!" Let the one who is thirsty come; and let the one who wishes to take *the free-gift of the water of life.*"

Praise Jesus. And yes, we must say free gift because so many refuse to accept and are unclear that it is just that. The "robes" referred to here are a symbol of "righteousness" and are to be washed in the blood of the Lamb of God as we accept and *believe* in Jesus yielding to us our salvation and redemption, gifted to us from our loving, providing Father God, through Jesus Christ our Lord, Savior, and Redeemer who came to glorify to the glory of Father God. Praise the Holy Spirit. Hallelujah! Amen.

This concludes the enumeration, purpose, and intended direction of this written composition to inform and promote or declare these truths that God has made known for our benefit and needs for our successful survival. I hope you have enjoyed the ride. Stay tuned, for there is more to come!

References

#1

The New Scofield Reference Bible.
Holy Bible Authorized King James Version.
One book or volume.
The Scofield Reference Bible, copyright 1909, 1917, copyright renewed.
1935, 1945, by Oxford University Press Inc. Copyright 1967.
City of publication: New York, NY.
Publisher: Oxford University Press.
Publication Date: Copyright 1st 1909, last 1967.

#2

Zondervan Publishing, Holy Bible.
NIV Holy Bible New International Version.
One book or volume.
Scripture Quotations taken from the Holy Bible, New International Version (NIV).
Copyright 1973, 1978, 1984, 2011 by Biblica Inc.
Used by permission. All rights reserved worldwide.
City of publication: Grand Rapids, Michigan.
Publisher: Zondervan.
Publication Date: 1st 1973, last 2011.

#3

Joseph Prince, Faithwords, Hatchette Book Group.
Live the Let-Go Life: Breaking Free From Stress, Worry, and Anxiety.
One book or volume.
Copyright 2018.
City of publication: New York, NY.
Hatchette Book Group Inc. Faithwords.
Publication Date: October 2018.

#4

Through the Bible with Les Feldick, Bible Instructor.
Through the Bible with Les Feldick.
Complete volume of Videos on YouTube under *Through the Bible with Les Feldick.*
Full catalog of videos on YouTube and at lesfeldick.net.
Fully self-published and distributed from 30706 W. Lona Valley Rd., Kinta, Oklahoma 74552.
Self-published by *Through the Bible with Les Feldick*, started television Bible ministry in 1990.

#5

The Zondervan Publishing House, *The New Compact Bible Dictionary.*
The New Compact Bible Dictionary, The Bible Handbook Series.
One volume only.
1st Edition Copyright 1967.
City of publication: Grand Rapids, Michigan.
Zondervan Publishing House.
Copyright 1967.

#6

American Bible Society.
The Holy Bible, The New King James Version.
One volume.
1st Edition.
City of publication: New York, NY.
Published by The American Bible Society.
Copyright 1967.

#7

Merriam-Webster Inc.
The New Merriam-Webster Dictionary.
One volume.
1st Edition 1989.
City of publication: Springfield, Massachusetts.
Published by Merriam-Webster Inc.
Copyright 1989.

8.

The Lockman Foundation.
The New Testament, Four Translation Parallel Edition.
King James Version 1611, revised 1963.
New American Standard Bible 1901.
Williams, *New Testament: In the Language of the People*, copyright 1937, renewed in 1964.
Beck, *New Testament: In the Language of Today*, copyright 1963, 5th printing 1965.
One volume.
Copyright 1963.
City of publication: La Habra, California.
Published by the Lockman Foundation.
Copyright 1963.

About the Author

Rick L. Johnson, sixty years old, is a Delaware native whose desire to glorify God manifested after his receiving of the knowledge of the Grace and Truth and Peace of Jesus Christ, exposing the error of many churches worldwide in their attempts to tie our "Gospel of Grace" to a performance-based economy, which is in direct opposition to the Word of God. This most vital and important piece of informational knowledge will transform lives and has called this *author* to share that message through this book and the founding of his Ricardo Da Vinci Ministries, a ministerial foundation to spread the news and to support, lift up, and lead people who are seeking the truth to their way home. Once this veil of misunderstanding is removed and the *love* of God is revealed in Jesus Christ, who is God's Grace personified, then the power begins to flow. Once we believe this, His Grace then begins to move in our lives. The number 5 is the number of "God's Grace." For that reason, there are five chapters in this book. The *Grace* of God has changed this author's life, and He has used God's Holy Bible to shore up affirm and confirm those assertions, using scriptures that instructed and moved him to a full understanding of Almighty God, or El Shaddai. As he reveals Jesus Christ, His deity, purpose, and power of His expressed love, here you will learn that we as believers are the righteousness of God in Christ Jesus. For clearly, He is the doorway.